P9-BIW-170

You're Gonna Be Alright Jamie Boy

David Freeman

copyright © 1974 David Freeman

published with assistance from the Canada Council

Talonbooks
201 1019 East Cordova
Vancouver
British Columbia V6A 1M8
Canada

This book was typeset by Beverly Matsu, designed by David Robinson and printed by Hemlock Printers for Talonbooks.

Second printing: November 1976

The cover photograph was taken by Robert A. Barnett.

Talonplays are edited by Peter Hay.

Rights to produce *You're Gonna Be Alright Jamie Boy*, in whole or in part, in any medium by any group, amateur or professional, are retained by the author, and interested persons are requested to apply to his agent, John Goodwin, 3823 Melrose Avenue, Montréal, Québec H4A 2S3, who is authorized to negotiate.

Canadian Shared Cataloguing in Publication Data

Freeman, David, 1945-
    You're gonna be alright Jamie boy

    ISBN 0-88922-066-2 pa.

    I. Title.
PS8561.R385 Y6 C812'.5'4
PR9199.3.F

CAMROSE LUTHERAN COLLEGE
LIBRARY

This is in the memory of television.

You're Gonna Be Alright, Jamie Boy was first performed at Tarragon Theatre in Toronto, Ontario, on January 12, 1974, as a co-production with Centaur Theatre, Montreal, P.Q., with the following cast:

Fran	Lillian Lewis
Jamie	David Ferry
Ernie	Hugh Webster
Carol	Jayne Eastwood
Fred	Stuart Gillard

Directed by Bill Glassco
Set Design by John Ferguson
Lighting by John J. Thomson
Sound by Richard Carson

I

Act One

JAMIE DINSDALE, a young man of about twenty-one, is sitting watching television, very lethargically. His mother, FRAN, enters, a woman in her fifties. She carries two bowls of potato chips. She looks at JAMIE, a little annoyed, and sets down the bowls.

FRAN:

Are you going to sit there all day? *No response.* I could use some help, you know.

Still no response. She gives an annoyed shrug and exits. In a few seconds she re-enters, carrying another bowl of chips.

Day in, day out, ever since you've come home. Nothing but sit and stare at that damn television. You keep that up, you'll wind up right back in the asylum.

JAMIE reaches over to steal a chip. FRAN smacks his hand.

FRAN:

> Not before dinner.

JAMIE:

> Institute.

FRAN:

> What?

JAMIE:

> Clarke Institute of Psychiatry.

FRAN:

> Different name. Same kind of people.

JAMIE:

> Why so many potato chips?

FRAN:

> Your father complained there weren't enough last time.

JAMIE:

> Well, if certain parties didn't pick them up by the fistfuls every five minutes, there'd be enough. By the way, Superstud is coming tonight, isn't he?

FRAN:

> If by that you mean Fred, yes, he is.

JAMIE:

> I thought Wednesday was his bowling night.

FRAN:

> Not anymore. He joined a new league over in the West End and they bowl Fridays. *Inspecting everything.* Oh God.

JAMIE:
What's wrong?

FRAN:
I forgot the peanuts.

JAMIE:
So?

FRAN:
Your father likes peanuts.

JAMIE:
He's also got the hots for Doris Day, Mom, but he's
not getting her tonight either.

FRAN:
Jamie, this is serious. He'll sulk and brood all night.

JAMIE:
Yeah, and treat you like a slave. It'll be last night
all over again.

FRAN:
Jamie, what are we going to do?

JAMIE:
No sweat. I'll run down and get some.

FRAN:
You can't. The store's closed by now.

JAMIE:
Then just tell him they were sold out.

FRAN:
But what if he checks?

JAMIE:

>He won't check.

FRAN:

>He might. Remember last time when I forgot the beer?

JAMIE:

>Mom, you gotta admit it was pretty dumb telling him Brewers Retail was all sold out.

FRAN:

>Boy, was he mad. He didn't speak to me for a whole week.

JAMIE:

>Why don't you just tell him to shove it?

FRAN:

>Be a good boy and get the beer out of the fridge.

JAMIE:

>Why? If I take it out now it'll get warm.

FRAN:

>Fred likes it warm. He says if it's too cold it loses flavour.

JAMIE:

>Fine. If Freddy boy wants a warm beer he can haul his ass down to the basement and get one.

FRAN:

>Just get the beer.

>*She switches off the TV.*

JAMIE:

>Alright, alright.

He exits to the kitchen.

FRAN starts to set up the TV trays.

JAMIE: *offstage*
>Tell me, Mom, do you really enjoy it?

FRAN:
>Enjoy what?

JAMIE:
>Family night.

FRAN:
>Well, your father seems to like it.

JAMIE: *entering*
>I'm not talking about Dad. I'm talking about you.

FRAN:
>Well sure, I enjoy it. Why not? We get to watch all those programs together. Besides, it's a chance to see Carol.

JAMIE:
>What kind of mood do you think she'll be in tonight? *Silence.* She was really upset on the phone this morning, wasn't she?

FRAN:
>You should have let me tell her where you were, Jamie.

JAMIE:
>She doesn't need me on her mind, Mom. She's got enough problems of her own. *Pause.* Enough beer?

FRAN:
> For now.

JAMIE:
> Mom, can we watch "Chariots of the Gods" tonight?

FRAN:
> What?

JAMIE:
> "Chariots of the Gods."

FRAN:
> What's that?

JAMIE:
> It's a documentary based on some guy's theory that the ancient gods were really astronauts.

FRAN:
> I thought you'd be past that stage by now.

JAMIE:
> What stage?

FRAN:
> You know, rockets, space monsters, stuff like that.

JAMIE:
> It's a very good documentary, Mom.

FRAN:
> Okay, what time is this thing on?

JAMIE:
> Seven o'clock.

FRAN:
> Seven o'clock! What about "Mod Squad?"

JAMIE:

>You see that every week.

FRAN:

>But Carol likes it. She likes that guy on it. Michael what's his name.

JAMIE:

>Mom, I'm not asking for much. I don't even like TV. I just want to watch this one thing.

FRAN:

>If it was any other night, I'd say okay, but this is family night and . . .

JAMIE:

>Screw family night! I don't give a shit about family night!

FRAN:

>Now, Jamie, don't get upset!

JAMIE:

>I'm not upset. *But he is.* Mom, just because I get angry, it doesn't mean I'm going off my rocker.

FRAN:

>I know that, dear. Look, we'll talk it over with your father when he gets home, okay? We'll let him decide. After all, it's his set.

JAMIE:

>It may be his set, but it was supposed to be my surprise.

FRAN:

>Surprise?

JAMIE:
Yeah, every time he came to the Clarke he kept hinting there was something waiting for me at home. Some surprise.

> *The sound of a door opening and closing is heard.*

ERNIE: *off*
Fran! Jamie! I'm home.

FRAN:
In here, Ernie.

> *ERNIE enters, a short but powerful looking man in his late fifties. He wears jeans, a plaid shirt and an old leather jacket. He carries a lunch pail. He also carries a parcel so large that he has to set it on the floor.*

JAMIE:
Hi, Dad. How's work?

ERNIE:
Oh, same old shit. *Noticing the beer.* There's a sight for sore eyes. Have one with me, boy?

JAMIE:
Sure.

FRAN:
Don't you two go getting drunk before dinner now.

ERNIE:
Jesus Christ, woman, the minute I get home! *Looking around.* Where are my nuts? *Silence.* Frances, where are my nuts?

FRAN:
Ernie . . .

ERNIE:
>   You forgot, didn't you? Goddamnit, woman, you'd
>   forget your head if it wasn't attached.

FRAN:
>   Ernie, I . . .

ERNIE:
>   You know I like nuts. I ask you specially, but you
>   forget. As usual.

JAMIE:
>   Dad, she didn't forget the nuts. I did.

ERNIE:
>   You?

JAMIE:
>   Yeah, me. I was going out for a walk and Mom
>   asked me to buy some peanuts, but it slipped my
>   mind.

ERNIE:
>   Slipped your mind, eh? Well, lucky I remembered.

>   *He opens up his lunch pail, pulls out a big bag
>   of peanuts and hands them to FRAN.*

>   Go put 'em in a dish. I want to talk to my son alone.

FRAN:
>   What's in the package?

ERNIE: *remembering*
>   Oh yeah, that . . . It's a little peace offering for last
>   night.

JAMIE:
>   Another one?

ERNIE: *unveiling it enthusiastically*
>There's a little cigar store about two blocks from the plant. They sell mostly crap, but this was in the window and I just couldn't pass it up.

>>*He unveils the ugliest plaster dog ever created. JAMIE and FRAN are stunned.*

FRAN:
>Nice.

ERNIE: *proudly*
>It's a dog.

JAMIE:
>Oh.

ERNIE:
>Well, whaddaya think, Fran? *No reply.* Fran? *Still no reply.*

JAMIE:
>She's speechless with delight.

ERNIE:
>For God's sake, woman, say something.

FRAN:
>I said it's very nice, dear.

JAMIE:
>How much did you pay for it?

ERNIE:
>Only seven-fifty.

JAMIE:
>Seven-fifty!

ERNIE:
Yeah, a real bargain, eh?

JAMIE:
Where are you gonna put it?

ERNIE:
Where am I gonna put it? I don't know. We can
leave it right here or we can put it in the bedroom.

FRAN: *alarmed*
Oh no! *Slight pause.* I mean, right here will be
fine.

ERNIE:
Okay, Fran, you've seen it, so shove off. I want to
have a talk with my son.

> *FRAN exits.*

JAMIE:
Dad, why buy a piece of junk like that?

ERNIE:
That isn't junk. Your mother likes things like that.

JAMIE:
No, she doesn't. She puts up with it, but she doesn't
like it.

ERNIE:
You don't know your mother. Before we were
married she'd have me down at Sunnyside Beach
every Saturday tossing those fucking baseballs till
my arm nearly fell off, just so's she could win a
Kewpie doll or a china horse.

JAMIE:
That was then. I'm talking about now.

19

ERNIE:

Well, I like them. They give the place class.

JAMIE:

Yeah, early brothel.

ERNIE:

Now don't you start with me, boy. I've got something important to talk to you about.

JAMIE:

Like what?

ERNIE:

Well, you know how Uncle Mo on "Bernie Loves Bridget" says, "Have I got a girl for you!"

JAMIE:

What's "Bernie Loves Bridget?"

ERNIE:

A television show.

JAMIE:

Never heard of it.

ERNIE:

Well, forget it. Listen, there's this girl in the office named Cindy, about twenty-two. Miniskirt, boobs, nice ass, everything a guy could want. We kid around a lot. Anyway, I showed her a picture of you and she got so excited I thought . . .

JAMIE:

Dad, please. Not again.

ERNIE:

Look, I'm doing you a favour. Do you want to get laid or don't you?

JAMIE:
Dad, I'm not interested.

ERNIE:
I got her phone number. I told her you'd call right after "Mod Squad."

JAMIE:
Why do you keep doing this to me?

ERNIE:
Why? Because it's unnatural for a boy your age not to be interested in girls, that's why.

JAMIE:
Look, Dad, I'm interested in girls, okay?

ERNIE:
Not enough for my liking. I want grandchildren.

JAMIE:
You're gonna have grandchildren.

ERNIE:
Yeah, sure, after eight years of marriage, Fred finally has a lucky night.

JAMIE:
So in six months you'll be a grandfather. What are you kicking about?

ERNIE:
It's not enough. I want to be a patriarch.

JAMIE: *laughing*
A patriarch!

ERNIE:
What's so damn funny? You two owe me that much.

JAMIE:
>Dad, did you decide this before or after you saw "The Waltons?"

ERNIE:
>Why can't I be a patriarch? Will Geer's one and he's happy as hell.

JAMIE:
>That's just a story, Dad. Make believe.

ERNIE:
>You tell that to Will Geer. You know he was drunk when he did it?

JAMIE:
>Will Geer, drunk?

ERNIE:
>No, dummy, your brother-in-law. At the rate he's going, old cocksure Fred, I'll have to get an extra job just to keep him in booze.

JAMIE:
>Well, he finally made it, didn't he? Give him credit for that.

ERNIE:
>Yeah, but can he do it again? I doubt it. They say once a night is enough. With Fred, once a year and he's ready for an oxygen tent. With two of you working on it, I'd have a chance.

JAMIE:
>What do you expect me to do, marry the first broad I meet?

ERNIE: *with absolute seriousness*
>No, just fuck her.

FRAN enters with a large dish of peanuts.

FRAN:
Here are your nuts. Discussion over?

ERNIE:
Not quite, but it can wait.

FRAN:
Did you tell your father about that "Chariot" thing yet?

ERNIE:
"Chariot" thing?

JAMIE:
It's not that important.

FRAN:
There's this program he wants to see about spacemen or chariots or something.

JAMIE:
I said it's not important.

ERNIE:
No, son, tell me more.

JAMIE:
Well, it's a special called "Chariots of the Gods." It's based on this guy's theory that the ancient gods were astronauts who came from other planets and were worshipped here by primitive societies.

ERNIE:
Sounds interesting.

FRAN:
It's on when "Mod Squad" is on.

ERNIE:

> So it won't hurt us to watch something different for
> a change. Ancient gods. Isn't that what they called
> the Italians in the olden days?

JAMIE:

> No, Dad, that was the Romans. Now the Romans
> had stories and legends that . . .

FRAN:

> Carol likes to watch "Mod Squad."

ERNIE:

> She can see it some other time.

JAMIE: *cautiously*

> Dad, it's ninety minutes long.

ERNIE:

> Ninety minutes! Oh well, there goes "Adam 12."

FRAN:

> Yeah, and the last of a two-parter too.

JAMIE:

> Forget it, Dad. I'll see it on the re-runs.

ERNIE:

> Oh no, if you're so hot about seeing it, you might as
> well see it now.

FRAN:

> He's right, Ernie. They'll re-run it and he can see it
> then.

ERNIE:

> Fran, I told him he could see it now.

FRAN:
> But Ernie, I . . .

ERNIE:
> Shut up!

JAMIE:
> Dad, you're being petty.

ERNIE:
> Who the hell's being petty? You want to see it so
> I'm letting you see it. Happy?

JAMIE:
> Dad, you can see "Adam 12."

ERNIE:
> Yeah, sure, and while I'm watching "Adam 12" you'll
> sit in the corner and pout.

JAMIE:
> Don't be ridiculous.

ERNIE:
> It'll be "Gunsmoke" all over again.

> *A bewildered pause.*

JAMIE:
> "Gunsmoke?"

ERNIE:
> Yeah, when Matt Dillon wouldn't let the trail hands
> drink in the saloon, they got mad and shot up the
> town and wounded poor old Doc.

JAMIE:
> I promise I won't shoot up the town.

ERNIE:

    Well, see that you don't. And while you're at it, go upstairs and get some proper clothes on.

JAMIE:

    Why?

ERNIE:

    Because we got company coming, that's why.

JAMIE:

    Dad, it's only Fred and Carol.

FRAN:

    Jamie, do as your father tells you.

> *JAMIE shrugs and exits. ERNIE goes back to his paper.*

    I talked to Carol on the phone this morning.

ERNIE:

    So?

FRAN:

    She was very upset.

ERNIE:

    What about?

FRAN:

    You know. Because we didn't tell her about Jamie.

ERNIE:

    Fran, it was better that she shouldn't know. We decided that, remember?

FRAN:

    I'm not so sure.

ERNIE:

Look, in her condition and with her problems I think we did the right thing. What did she say?

FRAN:

She accused us of not trusting her.

ERNIE:

Did you tell her it was my idea?

FRAN:

No.

ERNIE:

Well, there you go, you should have. There's no reason for you to take all the blame.

FRAN:

Well, I agreed to it. *Pause.* Ernie, what are we going to do about Carol and Fred?

ERNIE:

Nothing. It's their bed. Let them lie in it. *Pause.* You don't think Carol's been drinking again, do you?

FRAN:

As far as I know, not as heavily.

ERNIE:

Goddamnit, I told Fred not to let her drink at all!

FRAN:

Well, she may be drinking more than we know. Sometimes on the phone I can hardly understand her.

ERNIE:

Well that's just great for the baby, isn't it?

FRAN:

> Ernie, do you really think having this baby is going to solve all their problems?

ERNIE:

> I don't know. I thought it might start her caring a little.

FRAN:

> Well, I think the real problem is Fred.

ERNIE:

> Why? What's he done now?

FRAN:

> Nothing. That's the problem.

> *JAMIE enters. He has changed his clothes.*

ERNIE:

> Well, that's more like it. *Pause.* How've you been? What'd you do all day?

JAMIE:

> Watched television.

ERNIE:

> Anything else?

JAMIE:

> Read.

ERNIE:

> That a good book, son?

JAMIE:

> Not bad.

ERNIE:

> Trying to get information out of you is like pulling teeth. *To FRAN.* When he was a kid I couldn't get him to shut up.

JAMIE:

> Dad, what do you want from me?

ERNIE:

> Nothing. I don't want anything from you. What you gonna do tomorrow? Same as today?

JAMIE:

> Probably.

ERNIE:

> Figures.

> > *The doorbell rings.*

FRAN:

> That must be Carol and Fred.

> > *She exits.*

ERNIE:

> Late again as usual. Now listen Jamie, they don't know about the new TV. It's a surprise, so just keep your mouth shut and let them notice it.

JAMIE:

> Oh, for Chrissake, Dad.

ERNIE:

> Come on, it won't hurt you to be a sport for once, will it?

*FRED enters, a seedy looking slob of about thirty.
His once pretty fair physique is going to pot.
The face betrays a character that can be easily
led and terrorized and there is a sucky quality
about him.*

FRED: *sparring with ERNIE*
Eh, hey, hey, Dad.

ERNIE:
Have a beer, Fred?

FRED:
Don't mind if I do. Whaddaya say there, Jamie boy?

JAMIE: *unenthusiastically*
Fred.

*FRAN enters with CAROL. CAROL is a plain
girl of twenty-eight in her third month of
pregnancy. Her face is almost very hard with
the gentleness that was once there nearly gone.*

ERNIE: *embracing CAROL*
Well, hail, looks like the gang's all here.

CAROL:
Hi, Dad. *To JAMIE.*   Hi, kid. How ya doing?

JAMIE:
Hi, Carol.

ERNIE:
How you feeling, Carol?

CAROL:
Well, let's put it this way. I'll be glad when it's all
over.

FRED:

You're not even gonna have time to relax, Sugar, 'cause as soon as you have this one . . . *Making an obscene gesture.* We're gonna go at it again.

CAROL:

You think that's funny, do you, Fred? In mixed company?

There is an embarrassed silence.

FRED:

No, Sugar, I guess it wasn't.

CAROL:

Then why'd you say it? *Then, under her breath.* Stupid bugger.

Without waiting for an answer, she sits down beside JAMIE.

Thanks a lot for calling me.

JAMIE:

It wasn't that serious, Carol. Anyway, I didn't want to bother you.

CAROL:

What the hell do you mean, not serious? Jamie, a nervous breakdown is goddamn serious.

FRED: *showing false concern*

Yeah, guy, you really had us going there for a while. What happened anyway?

JAMIE:

I don't know. Strain, I guess.

CAROL:
Yeah, strain. I bet.

FRED:
You know what I think was the matter?

Everyone looks at FRED.

You see, I talked the whole thing over with Jock down at the garage and we both agree.

CAROL:
Fred, I really don't think Jamie needs an oil change.

FRED:
Very funny, Sugar. It's like this, Dad. Jock and me think it's too much studying and not enough hard work.

CAROL:
You don't think studying is hard work?

FRED:
I wouldn't know. I've been too busy busting my ass all my life like Dad here. Right, Dad?

ERNIE:
Right.

JAMIE:
I got news for you, Fred. Want to hear it?

FRED:
Shoot.

JAMIE:
Going to university is not a crime. Dig?

FRED:
>No, smart boy, I don't dig nothing. I'm a mechanic,
>not a ditch-digger.

JAMIE:
>Did I say you were?

CAROL:
>Fred.

ERNIE:
>Okay, you two, knock it off.

FRED:
>I'm just telling you what my buddy Jock found out,
>okay? People who read too much become neurotics
>and faggots. Just look at your English professors.

JAMIE: *incredulously*
>What?

CAROL:
>Okay, Fred, let's just cool it.

FRAN: *changing the subject, speaking to CAROL*
>How did things go today? Everything alright?

FRED: *quickly*
>The doctor says everything's just dandy, Mom.
>Carol's in real fine shape.

CAROL:
>If I wasn't pregnant, I'd be in even better shape, eh,
>Fred?

JAMIE:
>What do you mean?

FRAN:

Well, there's nothing easy about the third month. When I was having Jamie here, I practically lived in the bathroom.

ERNIE:

Yeah, and everytime I looked around, there she was, halfway down the toilet.

FRAN:

At least when *I* was sick I *made* it to the toilet.

ERNIE:

Yeah, yeah . . .

FRAN:

I didn't throw up all over the landlord's cat and get fined by the Humane Society.

ERNIE:

What are you talking about? I did *not* get fined by the Humane Society. The case was dismissed.

CAROL:

Why? What happened, didn't the cat show up to testify?

ERNIE:

No, goddamnit, it died. Now let that be the end of it.

FRAN:

Can I get you anything, Carol?

CAROL:

Yes, a scotch and soda.

ERNIE:

Not on your life, my girl. We're not having any of that nonsense again. Not in your condition —

CAROL:
> My condition's getting to be a real problem, isn't it, Fred? Can't have a drink, people won't tell me anything, everyone thinks they know better than the doctor. Well, let me tell you, Dad, having a kid ain't all it's cracked up to be. It's not all Flushabye commercials.

ERNIE:
> Aw, bullshit! It's a privilege to bear children. At least it was in my mother's day. She bore nine of 'em. Proud of it too.

JAMIE:
> Play it again, Sam.

ERNIE:
> What?

JAMIE:
> We've heard it all before, Dad.

ERNIE:
> That's what they teach you up at the big university, eh, boy? To sneer at old folks?

JAMIE:
> I wasn't sneering.

ERNIE:
> Well, I'd like to know what you'd call it. My mother is old folks.

JAMIE:
> She's also dead. Carol and I never knew her.

ERNIE: *angrily*
> Well, it would have been better for you if you had. She'd have made you two toe the mark. She was a

real pioneer lady like the kind you used to see on "Wagon Train." Not many women like that around nowadays.

FRAN:
No, not many women kill themselves in childbirth now. *To CAROL.* How about a ginger ale?

CAROL:
Okay, Mom.

FRAN exits to the kitchen. Pause.

ERNIE:
Carol, do you notice anything new?

CAROL:
You mean that thing?

She points to the dog

ERNIE:
Oh yeah, that too. How do you like it?

CAROL:
It's odious.

FRED:
Yeah, Sugar, I agree. Really nice, Dad.

CAROL:
What's it for?

ERNIE:
I bought it for Fran. Remind her of the old days at Sunnyside.

JAMIE:
The baseball bit, Carol.

CAROL:
>Oh yeah.

FRED:
>You used to play baseball, Dad?

ERNIE:
>Not exactly. There used to be an amusement park down where the Lakeshore highway is. I used to take the broads down there and knock over milk bottles with baseballs. Three throws for a dime. You shoulda seen me then, Fred. Solid as a rock.

FRED:
>Like me, eh?

CAROL:
>He said rock, Fred.

ERNIE:
>I had a physique as good as that guy in "Hawaii-Five-O." What's his name?

FRED:
>Jack Lord.

ERNIE:
>Yeah, Jack Lord. Used to look a little like him too.

FRED:
>Hey, Dad, remember when I used to play hockey?

CAROL: *cutting him short*
>So what else is new, Dad? Besides the dog?

ERNIE: *coyly*
>If you don't know, I'm not going to tell you.

CAROL:
> Fine. Jamie, when are you coming to see me?

ERNIE:
> Guess.

CAROL:
> Guess?

ERNIE:
> Yeah, come on now.

JAMIE:
> Dad, I think that . . .

ERNIE:
> I think that you just better keep your mouth shut.

CAROL:
> Why can't he tell me?

ERNIE:
> Because I want you to guess, that's why.

CAROL:
> Oh come on, this is silly.

ERNIE: *teasing*
> Guess or I'll send it back.

CAROL: *angrily*
> Dad, that's not funny.

ERNIE:
> Alright, then guess.

CAROL:
> Thursday?

ERNIE:
    Thursday?

CAROL:
    Friday?

ERNIE:
    What?

CAROL:
    Saturday? I don't know.

FRED:
    Is it bigger than a breadbox?

ERNIE: *thoroughly confused*
    What?

CAROL:
    If it's Saturday it'll have to be in the morning 'cause
    I'm going to the doctor's in the afternoon. What are
    you laughing at?

ERNIE:
    Wait a minute.

CAROL:
    I know what. Why don't you come with me to the
    doctor's?

ERNIE:
    Carol, what are you doing?

CAROL:
    I'm trying to guess when Jamie's coming to see me.

ERNIE:
    Wouldn't it be simpler just to ask him?

CAROL: *exasperated*
You told me to guess.

ERNIE:
I did not.

CAROL:
You did so!

FRED:
Is it round like a toilet bowl?

JAMIE:
Sure, I'll go to the doctor's with you. I'll come over tomorrow too if you like.

CAROL: *happy at the prospect*
Great, can you make it for lunch?

JAMIE:
Sure.

ERNIE:
Carol, there's something different about this room and I want you to guess what it is.

CAROL is stunned.

Well . . .

CAROL:
Well, what?

ERNIE:
Can you guess what's different about this room?

FRED:
Can you drink it?

CAROL:

Dad, why don't you just cut out the guessing games and tell us?

ERNIE:

Because this is more fun. Now you and Fred walk around the room and I'll tell you if you're cold or hot.

JAMIE:

Dad, why don't you just tell her?

CAROL:

Jamie's right. Why do we have to play these stupid games?

ERNIE:

Stupid. Stupid, are they? Okay, forget it, just forget it.

FRED:

You and your big mouth, Sugar. Now you've gone and hurt his feelings.

CAROL:

Okay, Dad, I'm sorry.

ERNIE:

A man comes home from a hard day's work, wants to relax and play with his kids. But no, they're too good to play with him.

CAROL:

Look, Dad, I said I was sorry. We'll play, okay?

ERNIE:

No, you don't want to.

CAROL:

Yes, I do. I looked forward to it all week.

She starts moving around the room.

CAROL:
　　Am I hot or cold?

ERNIE:
　　You're freezing. Fred, you're freezing too.

　　　　CAROL moves to the mantlepiece. JAMIE
　　　　directs FRED towards the hallway and FRED
　　　　exits in that direction. CAROL inspects some
　　　　objects on the mantlepiece.

　　You're still cold, Carol.

　　　　CAROL crosses to the chest, which is likewise
　　　　littered with knickknacks.

JAMIE: *as she crosses in front of the TV*
　　Dum-de-dum-dum . . .

ERNIE:
　　Jamie, shut up!

　　　　CAROL inspects the objects on the chest.

　　Fred, what the hell are you doing in the closet?

CAROL: *picking up an object*
　　These are new.

ERNIE:
　　Yeah, yeah, but you're still cold.

CAROL: *replacing it*
　　I see you've updated your garbage collection.

　　　　She crosses to the TV and looks at the objects
　　　　on top of the TV.

ERNIE:
> Carol! Carol, you're hot.

CAROL:
> Hot?

ERNIE:
> Yeah, you're hot!

CAROL:
> Fred, if I'm hot, what are you doing over there?

FRED:
> Why can't we both be hot?

CAROL:
> I've been trying to figure that out for the last eight years, honey.

> *She leans on the TV.*

ERNIE:
> Carol, you're boiling!

> *FRED comes rushing over.*

FRED: *picking up an object*
> Dad?

> *FRAN enters with a ginger ale.*

FRAN: *handing the glass to CAROL*
> Well, how do you two like our new television set?

ERNIE:
> Shit!

FRAN:
> What's wrong?

ERNIE:
>   Nothing. You just ruined my surprise, that's all.

FRAN:
>   What surprise?

CAROL:
>   Never mind, Mom.

FRAN:
>   You mean you were going to surprise them with
>   your new television set the way you surprised me
>   with your fishing pole last summer. *To the others.*
>   He put it over the edge of the bathtub and I nearly
>   sat on the hook.

ERNIE:
>   You should have!

FRED: *admiringly*
>   It's a real beaut, Dad. Is it colour?

ERNIE:
>   Of course it's colour. I bet you can't guess how
>   much I paid.

FRED:
>   No, how much?

ERNIE:
>   Guess.

FRED:
>   I dunno. About three hundred and fifty.

ERNIE:
>   Carol?

CAROL:
> A buck ninety-eight.

ERNIE:
> You're both wrong. Guess again.

CAROL:
> For Pete's sake, Dad.

ERNIE:
> Come on.

FRED:
> Four hundred dollars.

CAROL:
> A quarter and five box tops.

ERNIE:
> Quit being a smart ass.

FRED:
> How 'bout three hundred?

ERNIE: *exuberantly*
> Two hundred and twenty-five dollars on the nose.
> Is that a deal or is that a deal?

FRED:
> No kidding! How did you do it?

ERNIE:
> Simple. One of the guys put me on to this store on
> Dundas that deals in factory rejects. You know,
> sets that have something a little bit wrong with them
> but still work.

CAROL:
> Why did they reject this one?

FRAN:
>The faces all turn purple.

ERNIE:
>That's not why. The horizontal's a little loose. It acts up sometimes, especially in stormy weather. Have to give it a couple of good whacks on the side. But I still think I got a bargain.

JAMIE:
>There was no storm last night.

ERNIE:
>There must have been, Jamie, somewhere.

JAMIE:
>Maybe there was an earthquake in Outer Mongolia.

ERNIE:
>You forget, boy, that I bought this set to celebrate your coming home from the hospital.

JAMIE:
>Like hell.

ERNIE:
>A fat lot of good it did me too. Had to practically polish the screen with your ass to get you to notice it.

FRAN: *shocked*
>Ernie!

JAMIE:
>You bought that set because the Motorola was so broken down it couldn't be fixed anymore.

FRED:
>Never mind, Dad. You made one helluva deal.

ERNIE:
>   You bet I did.

FRED:
>   Though you might have made a better one if Jock
>   and I'd been along.

ERNIE: *feeling challenged*
>   Is that so now?

FRED:
>   Jock probably could have got that set for two
>   hundred or one hundred and fifty.

ERNIE:
>   How?

FRED:
>   Oh, Jock has his ways. Like this one time, Jock's
>   wife wanted a stereo so off goes Jock to the furniture
>   store, but he takes along this ring he got out of a
>   cereal box or something. It has a sharp edge, see.
>   Jock picks out the one he wants and then, when the
>   salesman isn't looking, he takes the ring and puts a
>   big scratch up the side of the cabinet. That knocked
>   off twenty-five bucks. Like I say, Jock has his ways.

CAROL:
>   So did John Dillinger.

FRED:
>   You going to a shrink now, Jamie?

JAMIE:
>   What's it to you?

FRED:
>   Just asking. I never had to go to one myself. Do
>   they have those long black couches like I'm always
>   seeing in the movies?

CAROL:
Mind your own business, Fred.

FRED:
I'm interested, Sugar.

CAROL:
Well, be interested in something else.

ERNIE:
Carol's right. Whatever happens between Jamie and
the shrink is confidential. *Pause.* By the way, you
had an appointment today. How'd ya get on?

FRAN:
Ernie!

ERNIE:
You didn't go discussing any of our personal affairs,
did you?

CAROL:
Dad, you just said Fred shouldn't ask . . .

ERNIE:
Well, we got a right to know. This is family.

FRAN:
Ernie, if the doctor's going to help him, Jamie's
going to have to be as honest with him as he can.

ERNIE:
Fran, honesty's one thing; gossiping's another. You
don't know doctors. They write books, go on talk
shows and God knows what else.

CAROL:
What's that got to do with anything?

ERNIE:
> I just don't want the whole world knowing things about us.

CAROL:
> What are you afraid of, Dad?

ERNIE:
> Nothing! I've been a good father and Jamie knows it.

CAROL:
> What sort of things are you talking about then?

ERNIE:
> Look, Carol, I won't have any shrink doctor making me go down there to answer a lot of embarrassing questions just so's he can twist things around and make it look like everything's my fault.

CAROL:
> Why would he do that?

ERNIE:
> Because they always try to put the blame on the father, that's why, and it's not fair. I've worked my ass off all my life and it's not fair.

> *Pause.*

FRED:
> All psychiatrists are faggots.

> *Everyone looks at FRED.*

CAROL:
> And who gave you that stunning piece of information, as if I didn't know?

FRED:
Jock did.

CAROL:
You know what old Jockstrap's full of.

FRAN:
Carol!

FRED:
Listen, Sugar, his name's Jock MacDougal, not
Jockstrap.

CAROL:
Maybe I should call him "The Piston." Isn't that
what he likes to be called?

FRED:
Look, I don't call your friends names, do I?

CAROL:
I don't *have* any friends, Fred!

There is an embarrassed silence.

FRED:
Anyway, there's two of them living next door to the
garage.

FRAN:
Psychiatrists?

FRED:
No, Mom, faggots.

JAMIE:
How do you know they're faggots?

FRED:

Because they're all white and puny and one of them walks like a flamingo.

JAMIE:

That doesn't make them faggots.

FRED:

Besides, one of them made a pass at Jock.

CAROL:

Oh, come on now, no one's that desperate.

FRED:

He did so.

ERNIE:

What did Jock do?

FRED:

He just showed them a picture of his wife and kid. Come to think of it, a picture of Jock's wife would scare anyone off. What a dog!

CAROL:

That's a terrible thing to say. The only nice thing about Jock is his wife.

FRED:

Nice is okay for other broads, Sugar, but us guys need something more. Right, Jamie?

JAMIE:

Depends on what you're looking for, Fred.

FRED:

So tell me, what do you look for?

JAMIE looks at FRED contemptuously.

51

FRAN:

> Well, I guess I'd better get those dinners in the oven.
> Who wants what?

ERNIE:

> I'll take beef.

JAMIE:

> Turkey's fine with me, Mom.

FRAN:

> With or without cranberry sauce?

ERNIE:

> You got a turkey dinner with cranberry sauce?

FRAN:

> Yes, and buttered squash.

ERNIE:

> What kind of dessert?

FRAN: *wearily*

> I don't know. Peach cobbler, I think.

ERNIE:

> I suppose that beef dinner has that soggy mint sauce
> that looks like someone pissed on it.

FRAN:

> Ernie, please!

ERNIE:

> And that muffin, so hard I chipped a tooth on it.

FRAN:

> Ernie, do you want the beef dinner or not?

ERNIE:
> Of course I do. You know it's my favourite.

JAMIE:
> Just plain turkey for me, Mom.

ERNIE:
> With or without cranberry sauce?

JAMIE: *pause*
> With. *Pause.* But without the peach cobbler.

ERNIE:
> What have you got against peach cobbler?

JAMIE:
> Nothing.

ERNIE:
> If you don't want your peach cobbler, can I have it?

JAMIE:
> I thought you only liked raspberry strudel.

ERNIE:
> I do, but I thought I'd try something different for a change.

JAMIE:
> Fine. Mom, bring me a turkey dinner with everything and Dad will have the peach cobbler.

FRAN:
> Okay, it's turkey for Jamie, beef for Ernie. Carol, what'll you have?

CAROL:
> Is there any chicken, Mom?

FRAN:
    Yes.

CAROL:
    Then I'll have that.

ERNIE:
    Forget the beef dinner, Fran. Just make me a cheese
    sandwich.

FRAN:
    What?

ERNIE:
    I just want a cheese sandwich.

FRAN: *just short of being furious*
    Look, Ernie, first you wanted beef and then you
    started this whole silly interrogation about the
    turkey and now all you want is a cheese sandwich?

ERNIE:
    Yeah.

JAMIE:
    Dad, do you want the turkey with cranberry sauce?

ERNIE:
    It's alright. Let no man accuse me of taking food
    from the mouths of my own children.

JAMIE:
    Oh, for Chrissake!

FRAN:
    Ernie, there are two turkey dinners with cranberry
    sauce.

54

ERNIE:

Well, why the hell didn't you say that in the first place?

FRAN:

You didn't give me a chance.

ERNIE:

Goddamn woman thinks I'm a mind reader.

FRAN:

Do you want turkey with cranberries or not?

ERNIE:

No, you know I don't like turkey. All I want is the cranberry sauce.

FRAN:

Why didn't you tell me?

ERNIE:

You didn't ask me. No one asks me anything around here.

FRAN:

Okay, Jamie, you're going to have the turkey, Ernie will have the beef with cranberry and mint sauce and Carol . . .

CAROL:

I'm having chicken, Mom.

FRED:

As usual.

CAROL:

What's that supposed to mean?

FRED:
> It means you always get the chicken and I'm always stuck with that chow mein shit.

CAROL:
> I thought you liked the chow mein shit.

FRAN:
> Carol!

CAROL:
> I mean, the chow mein. I always buy it for you.

FRED:
> Yeah, and you always buy the chicken for yourself, don't you, Sugar?

CAROL:
> Well, I always give you my apple crisp.

FRED:
> FUCK THE APPLE CRISP!

ERNIE:
> Now you just hold it right there, boy!

FRED:
> Sorry, Dad.

CAROL:
> Are there two chicken dinners, Mother?

FRAN:
> No, just one.

CAROL:
> Then you'd better give that one to Freddy. I wouldn't want to deprive the poor boy. By the way, Mom, what are you having?

FRAN:

    Shrimp.

CAROL:

    Don't you like chicken too?

FRAN: *resenting what CAROL is leading up to*

    Carol, I'm happy with the shrimp.

CAROL:

    If I'd known there was only one chicken, I wouldn't
    have asked for it.

FRED:

    Carol.

CAROL:

    What is it, Freddikins?

FRED:

    She can have the stinkin' dinner.

CAROL:

    Oh, no, Lammy-pie, it's first come, first served,
    especially when you're first.

FRED: *threateningly*

    Cut it out, Sugar.

CAROL:

    Or else what? Tell me, Freddy, I'm tremendously
    interested.

    FRED says nothing.

    Maybe you should consult Jockstrap and find out
    what to do next.

    FRED glares at her.

FRAN:

Carol, why don't you come into the kitchen and make coffee while I get the dinners ready.

CAROL and FRED look at each other for a moment, then CAROL exits to the kitchen.

Does everyone want soup to start with?

ERNIE:

What kind of soup?

FRAN:

Vegetable. Any objections?

They shake their heads.

Fine.

FRAN exits to the kitchen.

ERNIE:

Say, Fred, what's wrong between you and Carol?

FRED:

What do you mean?

ERNIE:

You're on each other's backs all the time. How come?

FRED:

Well, you know women, Dad. They act kind of stupid when they get pregnant.

ERNIE:

You sure there's nothing wrong?

CAMROSE LUTHERAN COLLEGE
LIBRARY

FRED:

I'm positive.

ERNIE:

Still as happy as ever?

FRED:

I guess so.

ERNIE:

You don't sound very convinced.

JAMIE:

For Pete's sake, Dad. What do you want, a sworn affidavit?

ERNIE:

You keep quiet. You don't even take out girls. By the way, when are you gonna call little Cindy?

JAMIE:

Little who?

ERNIE:

Cindy Lovett, the girl I've been chatting up for you all week.

JAMIE:

You don't have to chat up anyone for me, Dad.

ERNIE:

Well, the fact is I already have. And I promised her you'd call her tonight.

FRED:

Who's Cindy?

ERNIE:

> A little number that came to work in the office last month. Red hair, cute little ass and the loveliest pair of knockers you ever laid your eyes on.

FRED:

> Sounds great. She could park her shoes under my bed anytime.

> *ERNIE glares at him.*

> If I wasn't so happily married to Carol. What's stopping you, Jamie, she sounds like a real winner?

JAMIE:

> Maybe we should enter her in the Kentucky Derby.

ERNIE:

> Don't be a smart ass. When are you gonna call her?

JAMIE:

> I told you when. Never.

FRED:

> C'mon, you can't keep hanging around with guys.

JAMIE:

> I don't hang around with guys.

ERNIE:

> Jamie, she's expecting to hear from you. It'll only take you a minute.

JAMIE: *to ERNIE*
> Why don't you call her yourself?

ERNIE:

> Well, because . . .Aw, to hell with you. *Turning to FRED.* So how are you keeping, Fred? How's the new job?

FRED:

> It's hardly new, Dad. I've been working there since Christmas.

ERNIE:

> You know, it beats me how you can give up a perfectly good job as an assistant foreman to go work in a garage.

FRED:

> I like working on cars, Dad.

ERNIE:

> Yeah, but at least at the plant you were giving orders, not taking them. Except, of course, from me.

FRED:

> Well, I may not be taking orders much longer.

ERNIE:

> Why? Has Jock been talking about the partnership again?

FRED:

> He hinted at it a couple of times last week. Nothing's settled yet though. Jock's got a lot on his mind, you know. The garage has only been open a year.

ERNIE:

> Well, I'll say this, you're really missed up there at the plant, boy, really missed. There's no one to have a beer with after work anymore.

JAMIE:

> There are other guys at the plant, Dad.

ERNIE:

> Those shitheads? They never forgave me for being promoted over their heads. Take Sweeney, for

instance. You remember Sweeney, don't you, Fred? Short little fart with glasses, partly bald. Reminds me of that private eye on TV. What's his name? Jamie, what's his name?

JAMIE:

How should I know?

ERNIE:

Oh, I forgot. Big college men don't watch television. Cannon! That's it. Cannon.

FRED:

Oh, Sweeney!

ERNIE:

Yeah, Sweeney. Anyway Sweeney and I started going for a beer together after work the way you and I used to. Then, just when I think it's gonna be a regular thing, all of a sudden he's too busy. He's gotta rush home for supper 'cause he's taking his wife to the movies.

JAMIE:

Maybe he was.

ERNIE:

Movies, my ass. It was jealousy. Or else those other vindictive bastards got to him. Probably threatened to kick him off the bowling team for kissing the foreman's ass. Old four-eyes Sweeney, so easy to push around. Even if the part about his wife was true, he could have taken her out another night. I'm getting even with the fucker though. He's out on the loading dock this week, freezing his nuts off. *Pause.* Do you know, Fred, I even offered to give that little bastard my bowling ball?

FRED:

Whaddaya mean? Don't you play anymore?

ERNIE:
    Hell, no. I quit after you left.

FRED:
    Why?

ERNIE:
    Well, what was the point? I mean, I only joined
    because you did. I don't particularly enjoy playing
    with a lot of jealous sons-of-bitches who secretly
    hate my guts.

    FRED nods. There is an embarrassed silence.

FRED:
    I wonder what's on the old boob tube?

ERNIE:
    Fred, how does Carol feel about you being a
    mechanic?

FRED:
    Well, you know women, Dad. They don't care what
    the hell you do, as long as you bring home the bacon.

ERNIE:
    True enough. I bet they sure miss you on that
    bowling league though. You were the only one that
    could bowl worth a shit. You should have seen this
    bastard, Jamie. Sometimes four or five strikes in a
    row.

FRED:
    Well, what are we gonna watch tonight, "Mod Squad?"

ERNIE:
    No, Fred, tonight we're gonna get educated. Jamie
    here wants to see something called "Chariots of the
    Gods."

FRED:
> Who?

ERNIE:
> Some crap about Italian astronauts.

JAMIE:
> It's not about Italian astronauts and I told you you could watch "Adam 12."

ERNIE:
> No, Jamie, we wouldn't expect a big college man like you to be interested in things like "Mod Squad" and "Adam 12," even if it is the last of a two-parter.

JAMIE:
> Look, if you want to see "Adam 12," see the bloody thing!

FRED:
> I don't care what you see as long as it's over by eight o'clock.

ERNIE:
> What happens at eight o'clock?

FRED:
> Hockey game.

ERNIE:
> Oh hell, is that on tonight?

FRED:
> Yeah, I guess so, it's the playoffs.

ERNIE:
> Well, you can't.

FRED:

    Why the hell not?

ERNIE:

    Because tonight is "Columbo" night. And Fran likes to see that.

FRED:

    "Columbo?"

ERNIE:

    Yeah. You know that little wop cop who goes around solving murders and crap like that?

FRED:

    Dad, it's the playoffs!

ERNIE:

    Why can't you listen to it on the radio?

FRED:

    In that case we might as well go home. Carol!

ERNIE:

    Now wait a minute . . .

FRED:

    Dad, I've been listening to the game on the radio all week. I thought tonight I was gonna see it. You're letting Jamie watch that "Chariot" shit.

ERNIE:

    That's different.

FRED:

    How different?

ERNIE:

    Well, Jamie's just come home.

FRED:

> Dad, I work my ass off all week. I was looking forward to this.

ERNIE: *calling*

> Fran! *Pause.* Fran!

FRAN: *off*

> Later, Ernie, I'm busy.

ERNIE:

> No, now. This is important.

> *FRAN enters.*

FRAN:

> Well?

ERNIE:

> Do you really want to see "Columbo" tonight?

FRAN:

> Do I? . . . Why?

ERNIE:

> Because Fred wants to see the hockey game. It's the playoffs.

FRAN:

> Fine.

ERNIE:

> What's fine?

FRAN:

> Fred can see the hockey game.

ERNIE:

> You don't mind missing "Columbo?"

66

FRAN:

> No.

ERNIE:

> You sure?

FRAN:

> Ernie, I got soup on the stove.

> *She exits to the kitchen.*

ERNIE:

> There, all settled.

FRED:

> I'm not putting Mom out, am I?

ERNIE:

> No, she can see the little slob another time. Jeez, don't you ever get tired of watching hockey? What's wrong with your TV anyway?

FRED:

> Oh, the tube blew up again. You know, Dad, I used to play centre when I was a kid in Kingston. I was gonna make a career of it.

JAMIE:

> Being a kid in Kingston?

FRED:

> No, hockey. Our team was called the Thunderbolts, remember, Dad?

ERNIE:

> Yes, Fred, you told me.

FRED:

> There was one season there I scored more goals than anyone. About four hundred.

JAMIE:

> Four hundred! Come off it.

FRED:

> Whaddaya mean, come off it, I once shook hands with Howie Meeker.

JAMIE:

> No kidding. I bet he didn't wash his hands for a whole week.

FRED:

> I remember this one game, Dad. We were playing about an hour overtime. The score was two all. Anyway, the Popeyes got the puck and . . .

JAMIE:

> The Popeyes?

FRED:

> Yeah, that's what they called themselves. They got the puck, you see, and started down the ice and all of a sudden . . .

JAMIE:

> Olive Oyl throws the captain a can of spinach.

ERNIE:

> Shut up, Jamie. Go on, Fred.

FRED:

> Wait. I'll show you. Let's see, that chair can be the goal and you two be the defencemen. Dad, you stand there.

> *He places ERNIE on one side of the chair.*

> And Jamie, you park your butt over here.

JAMIE:
Why can't you just tell us, Fred?

ERNIE:
Get off your ass, Jamie. It won't hurt you to
co-operate.

*JAMIE allows himself to be placed on the other
side of the chair.*

FRED:
Now I need a stick and a puck.

*He exits to the hall for a few seconds and comes
back with an umbrella.*

Stick.

ERNIE: *nodding agreement*
Stick.

FRED picks up a bottle cap.

FRED:
This is the puck.

ERNIE:
A bit small, isn't it?

FRED:
It's a demonstration model.

ERNIE: *to JAMIE*
Oh well, could have been worse. He could have used
a potato chip.

FRED:
Come on, Dad, that would crumble. *Laughing.* Get
it?

They wince.

FRED:

Now I'm gonna try to put the puck under the chair

> *He tries and they successfully block him. He tries again and again, they block him. He tries again.*

Jamie, you're not doing it right!

JAMIE: *still blocking him*
You said to block you.

> *JAMIE, ERNIE and FRED are now engaged in a shoving match. Exasperated, FRED drops the umbrella and puts up his dukes.*

FRED:

Alright, the game is hockey, not Kung Fu!

> *JAMIE and ERNIE play innocent.*

Hey, where's the puck?

JAMIE:

Bottle cap.

FRED:

Have it your way, but where is it?

ERNIE:

Probably under the sofa.

FRED:

No, it's not there. What the hell happened . . .

> *JAMIE moves and FRED spots the puck.*

FRED:

Jamie, you were standing on it! Okay, let's try once more.

JAMIE:

Oh, come on, Fred.

ERNIE:

Jamie's right. Enough's enough. I's starting to feel like a horse's ass.

FRED:

What's the matter with you guys? You chicken?

ERNIE and JAMIE take their places and the make believe hockey game begins all over again FRED is again blocked successfully. This time JAMIE deliberately pushes FRED over. Just then, CAROL and FRAN enter each carrying two bowls of hot soup.

FRAN:

What are you doing on the floor, Fred?

JAMIE:

I pushed him.

FRAN:

What for?

JAMIE:

He was trying to put a bottle cap under the chair.

FRAN:

Bottle caps belong in waste paper baskets, not under chairs.

FRED:

I was using it for a puck.

FRAN:

>I don't care what you were using it for. I just vacuumed this floor.

CAROL:

>What are you doing with Mom's umbrella?

FRED:

>Using it for a hockey stick.

ERNIE:

>Fred's been telling us about the time he used to play hockey.

FRAN:

>That's a good umbrella. I paid a lot for it.

>*She takes it and puts it away.*

CAROL:

>Did he also tell you about the time he scored a goal on his own net?

FRED: *angrily*

>Who told you that?

CAROL:

>Here's your soup, Lammy-pie. Jock did, your bosom buddy.

FRED:

>Jock's full of shit.

CAROL:

>Precisely. Whenever Jock talks about anyone else, he's the soul of truth, but whenever he talks about you, he's full of shit.

FRAN:
> Carol!

CAROL: *as FRED tries to sit down beside her*
> Sit over there.

FRED:
> That goal was an accident.

CAROL:
> Almost got you kicked off the team, especially when
> you did it twice in the same period.

FRED:
> Listen, Sugar, it may interest you to know that the
> coach once said the Leafs could use a man like me.

CAROL:
> Sure, playing for Boston. Are you going to watch
> "Columbo" tonight, mother?

FRAN: *annoyed that CAROL is trying to start trouble*
> You know I'm not.

CAROL:
> Why? I thought it was your favourite program.

FRAN:
> I'll see it another night.

FRED:
> We're gonna watch the hockey game. Any objections?

CAROL:
> I wonder if Gordie Howe's mother-in-law has to
> make such sacrifices.

ERNIE: *firmly*
> Carol.

73

CAROL:
What?

ERNIE:
Just calm down, okay?

CAROL:
I am calm, Dad. It's just that I know how much mother likes Peter Falk and I hate to see her miss him.

ERNIE:
Carol, *I* want to see the hockey game.

CAROL:
Since when have you been so crazy about hockey?

ERNIE: *putting his foot down*
Since tonight. *Looking at his watch.* Jamie, it's almost time for your ancient gods crap.

JAMIE:
Look, for the hundredth time, I don't want to see "Chariots of the Gods."

ERNIE:
Yes you do or you wouldn't have brought it up.

CAROL:
What about "Mod Squad?" Aren't we going to watch "Mod Squad?"

ERNIE:
No, we're gonna watch a piece of turd about ancient gods being astronauts.

FRED:
Ancient gods. You mean like fairies.

CAROL:
>But we always see "Mod Squad."

ERNIE:
>Well, I'm missing "Adam 12."

JAMIE: *shouting, almost out of control*
>See "Mod Squad." See "Adam" fucking "12." See
>any goddamn thing you want. Only stop badgering
>me. Please stop badgering me.

ERNIE:
>Who's badgering?

FRAN: *angrily*
>You are, Ernie Dinsdale. Sometimes I don't think
>you've got a brain in your head or a sensitive bone
>in your body.

ERNIE:
>Don't you shout at me, woman!

FRAN:
>I will so shout at you. Can't you realize that boy's
>been sick? Mentally ill!

>*ERNIE looks around shamefaced.*

CAROL:
>Jamie, I'm sorry. Please don't get upset. I can see
>"Mod Squad" anytime.

ERNIE:
>That's right, son. If you want to see "Chariots of
>the Gods," we're gonna see it. Like I said, it won't
>hurt us to watch something different for a change.

FRED:

Yeah, I really like those space shows. Boy, do I miss that "Starlost." Remember "Starlost?" What channel is it on?

JAMIE:

Stop patronizing me.

ERNIE:

No one's patronizing you, son. The man's just asking you a question.

JAMIE:

Channel nine.

FRED turns it on.

CAROL:

Here, Jamie. Sit down beside me and eat your soup.

He does.

ERNIE:

Say, Jamie, this thing hasn't got subtitles, has it?

JAMIE:

No, Dad, it's dubbed.

FRED:

There, just starting.

He pulls his chair in front of the TV, blocking FRAN's view.

FRAN:

Fred, I can't see. *Pause.* Fred, I can't see! *Pause.* Fred!

CAROL:

> Move your ass, you stupid bugger, you're not transparent, you know.

> *FRED moves his chair. He is now blocking ERNIE's view.*

ERNIE:

> Why don't you climb inside the goddamn thing!

> *No reaction from FRED, who is glued to the TV.*

CAROL:

> If we wanted to count your curls, Goldilocks, we wouldn't have turned the set on.

FRED: *turns to ERNIE*
> What's she yapping about?

CAROL:

> Excuse me please, I'll handle this.

> *She gets up and moves FRED to another chair.*

FRED:

> All you had to do was say something.

THE OTHERS:

> Sssshhhh . . .

> *Silence while they all watch TV.*

FRAN:

> The faces are all purple.

ERNIE:

> Fred, adjust the colour and the contrast, will you?

FRED does so.

FRED:
> Best I can do, Dad.

ERNIE:
> That's fine, Fred, just fine.

FRAN:
> Now they're pink.

ERNIE:
> Frances, haven't you ever heard of sunburn?

CAROL:
> On cactus?

> *Static noise is heard coming from the TV set.*

FRED:
> It's acting screwy, Dad.

ERNIE:
> I can see that. Jiggle the horizontal.

> *FRED does so.*

FRED:
> It won't work.

ERNIE:
> Give it a bang on the side then.

> *FRED gives it a good bang.*

ERNIE:
> Hey, take it easy! It's not a punching bag.

FRED:

> Is that better?

FRAN:

> Wow, that's the best the colour's ever been.

ERNIE:

> Ssh! I'm trying to hear this.

> *They watch for a moment.*

FRED:

> Pass the potato chips, Sugar.

CAROL:

> You still have your soup, Fred.

FRED:

> I want potato chips too.

CAROL:

> Not with soup, stupid!

ERNIE:

> Goddamnit, Carol, give him the potato chips and
> stop arguing. I'm trying to watch this.

> *She hands over the potato chips. As they watch
> the program, it is clear that they are all
> escaping reality, especially ERNIE. This most
> telling silence should last at least fifteen seconds.
> They all sit mesmerized by the television. Their
> movements are subtle, taking potato chips,
> eating their soup, etc. The interlude should tell
> how important TV is to this family and show
> how they place it above everything else — with
> the possible exception of JAMIE. The scene
> should continue until the commercial, at which
> point they all relax.*

ERNIE: *examining his soup*
    Fran, what's in this soup?

FRAN:
    Vegetables. What did you expect to find in
    vegetable soup, meatballs and spaghetti?

ERNIE:
    That canned shit again. I don't remember when I saw
    so much as a fresh carrot in this place.

FRAN:
    Ernie, the last time there was a fresh carrot in this
    house, it rotted because you were sick of "Bunny"
    food.

ERNIE:
    There's no bread either.

FRAN: *exasperated*
    Oh, God.

      She exits.

ERNIE: *loudly*
    Well, for Chrissake, Fran, it wouldn't be a bad idea
    to set the table once in a while.

FRAN: *off*
    I've only got two hands, Ernie.

ERNIE:
    You could get off your ass and start a little earlier.

CAROL:
    Have you ever considered giving her a hand, Dad?

      JAMIE gets up and starts to turn the channel.

80

ERNIE:
>What do you think you're doing?

JAMIE:
>Turning it to "Mod Squad."

ERNIE:
>Just leave it where it is. I found that interesting.

>>*JAMIE shrugs and goes back to his seat.*

FRED:
>There it goes again.

ERNIE:
>It's that damned horizontal.

>>*FRED gets up to fix it. JAMIE joins him and they start arguing.*

CAROL: *singing*
>Don't know why
>There's no sun up in the sky
>Stormy weather.

ERNIE:
>Alright, get out of the way.

>>*ERNIE pushes FRED and JAMIE aside and starts fiddling with knobs. He slaps the set a couple of hard blows. Finally, in exasperation, he starts kicking it. FRAN enters carrying a basket of bread.*

FRAN:
>Ernie! What are you doing?

ERNIE: *still kicking the TV*
>Goddamned TV won't come in.

FRAN:
>Well, kicking it won't do any good.

FRED:
>Could be a tube.

ERNIE:
>How can it be a tube? It's a brand new set.

JAMIE:
>It's a factory reject.

ERNIE:
>They guy told me it was the best one in the place.

>>*He fiddles frantically with the dials again, slapping it as he does so.*

CAROL:
>He also ripped you off for two hundred and twenty-five bucks.

ERNIE:
>Gimme the phone book.

FRAN:
>What for?

ERNIE:
>Never mind, just give it to me. *As she goes to fetch the phone book.* The yellow pages.

>>*She brings in the yellow pages and hands them to FRED.*

>Fred, look up TV repairmen.

FRAN:
>Ernie, it's late. No one's going to come out at this hour.

ERNIE:

What are you talking about? Some of them are open all night.

FRAN:

It'll cost you a fortune. You know what they charge for overtime. Besides, they probably won't get here till eleven.

ERNIE:

Good. Just in time for the late show.

FRED:

What about the hockey game?

ERNIE:

What about it?

FRED:

Dad, if I can't see the hockey game, I'm going home.

CAROL:

Oh, before or after your chicken dinner?

FRED:

Don't start with me again, Sugar!

ERNIE:

Just relax, Fred, and give me a number to call. We'll get the damn thing working.

FRED shows him a number. He moves to the phone.

222-3532, 222-3532, 222-3532, 222-3532 . . .

CAROL: *to JAMIE*

On Saturday morning, he won't eat his Rice Krispies until he's see "Huckleberry Hound."

FRED:
I'm warning you, Carol!

CAROL:
Oh, it's threats now, is it, Freddy? Well, I might just start making a few threats myself.

JAMIE:
What are you talking about?

CAROL:
Fred knows.

FRAN:
Alright you two, that's enough. Now let's everyone just calm down and we'll have dinner. Jamie, come and help me dish up.

JAMIE and FRAN exit to the kitchen.

FRED: *turning down the TV*
What's happening, Dad?

ERNIE: *on the phone*
No answer.

CAROL:
Speaking of answers, I'd like a few myself, Dad.

ERNIE: *putting down the receiver*
Like what?

CAROL:
Like why did Jamie land in the Clarke and why the hell wasn't I told about it?

FRED:
I told you, Sugar, we didn't want to upset you.

CAROL:
>And that's another thing. Why did you tell Fred and not me? You never tell me anything.

ERNIE:
>Keep your voice down, he'll hear you.

CAROL:
>Then tell me what's wrong with him. Why did he have the breakdown?

ERNIE:
>Look, he told you himself, it was strain. Ask the doctors if you don't believe me.

CAROL:
>That's bullshit! You were running up there every weekend. You know what happened. Now tell me, for Chrissake, I have a right to know!

ERNIE:
>Nothing happened. What the hell are you trying to say?

>*FRAN and JAMIE enter with the TV dinners.*

FRAN:
>Did you get the repairman, dear?

ERNIE:
>No, I'll try again after dinner.

JAMIE: *as he hands him his dinner*
>I've got bad news for you, Dad. Guess what? The landlord's cat ate your peach cobbler.

>*Blackout.*

Act Two

*About twenty minutes later. The TV dinners
have been eaten and the trays and coffee
cups are lying around. ERNIE is on the phone
and FRED is kneeling in front of the TV,
fooling with the dials. FRAN starts to clean
up.*

ERNIE:

That's right, 99 Green Street. *Long pause.* Whaddaya mean, it's out of your jurisdiction? Look, your
ad says "All Night TV Repair," it doesn't say anything about that. *Pause.* Well, if you don't come
my handicapped kid's gonna miss his favourite TV
program. *Pause.* He's blind. *Pause.* He's a good
listener. *Pause.* Whaddaya mean, twenty-five bucks?
Shove it up your ass!

He slams down the receiver.

FRAN:

Ernie! That's no way to talk on the telephone.

87

ERNIE:

>Goddamn repairmen! Next thing they'll be wanting you to send limousines.

JAMIE: *holding the telephone book*

>Well, compared to the last four we tried, it's cheap. Want to try another one?

ERNIE:

>No.

CAROL:

>Well, that's that. *Getting up.* Get the coats, Fred.

>*FRED starts toward the hall.*

ERNIE:

>Get the coats? Where's everybody going?

CAROL:

>Home.

ERNIE:

>Home? It's only seven-thirty. I thought you wanted to watch the hockey game.

CAROL:

>How is Fred going to watch a hockey game on a TV set that's broken?

ERNIE:

>Well, if someone gets a screwdriver, maybe Fred can fix it. Whaddaya say, Fred?

CAROL:

>Fred's a grease-monkey, not an electrician.

FRED:

>The word's mechanic, Sugar. Where's that screwdriver, Dad?

ERNIE:
> Fran, get a screwdriver.

FRAN:
> Ernie, you don't know anything about fixing a television and neither does Fred.

ERNIE:
> Do as I say, woman!

> *She exits quickly.*

JAMIE:
> Why can't you wait and call the repairman tomorrow?

ERNIE:
> Because the hockey game is on tonight. Besides, I don't want to pay some joker fifteen bucks just for turning a lousy screw.

JAMIE:
> You two may bugger it up more than it is already. You don't even know what you're looking for.

ERNIE:
> Fred does, don't you, Fred?

CAROL:
> Fred doesn't know the difference between a picture tube and a spare tire.

FRED:
> Whaddaya mean?

CAROL:
> I mean, don't go lousing this one up the way you did ours. He short-circuited the bloody thing with a fountain pen and blew the main fuse.

FRED:

I did not. The pen wasn't long enough. It was your stupid nail file.

ERNIE:

Alright you two, clam up!

FRAN enters with the screwdriver. ERNIE takes it and examines it carefully.

FRAN:

Now what's wrong?

ERNIE:

Nothing. It'll do, I guess.

He hands the screwdriver to FRED, who begins unscrewing the back of the set.

While we're waiting, why don't you call up little Cindy?

JAMIE:

I don't think so.

ERNIE:

Who's it gonna hurt? You call up and say hello, ask for a date.

CAROL:

Who's Cindy?

ERNIE:

Girl who works in the office up at the plant. Real excited about meeting Jamie.

FRAN: *annoyed*

Starting that again, are we?

90

ERNIE:
Starting what again?

FRAN:
Jamie's perfectly capable of finding his own girls,
Ernie.

ERNIE:
When?

CAROL:
I don't think that's any concern of yours, Dad.

ERNIE:
Look, what's wrong with trying to introduce my son
to a nice broad, I mean girl?

CAROL:
Dad, if you're so hot about this nice broad, why
don't you date her yourself?

ERNIE:
Now you're talking nonsense.

CAROL:
I'm sure Mom wouldn't mind.

FRAN:
It'd be a nice change from bowling.

ERNIE:
Besides, she's not a broad, she's a lady. A real little
lady.

JAMIE:
So is Mom.

> *By now FRED has the back of the TV off and
> is peering into it.*

FRAN:

> Ernie, why are you so anxious for him to call her?

ERNIE:

> Fran, will you just keep out of this.

FRED:

> Gee, I wish I'd had an old man who set me up with the broads.

CAROL:

> Fred, just shut up and fix the television.

ERNIE:

> See anything?

FRED:

> Not a damn thing. No loose wires, nothing. Sure is dusty for a set that's supposed to be brand new.

ERNIE:

> Could that have anything to do with it?

FRED:

> I doubt it.

ERNIE:

> Well, let's not take any chances. Fran, get a cloth and we'll dust it out.

FRAN:

> Ernie, what could dust possibly have to do with it not working?

ERNIE:

> Goddamn it, woman, sometimes you act just like Edith Bunker. Now do as I say!

FRAN:

> Okay, Archie.

She exits.

CAROL:

> Why can't you get your own rag? Mom's been up and down like a yoyo ever since we got here.

ERNIE:

> Well, who's fault is that? She should organize herself better.

CAROL:

> How the hell can she organize herself for something like this?

ERNIE:

> Lots of women do it. Look at Florence Henderson in "The Brady Bunch" or Harriet Nelson in "Ozzie's Girls." They're prepared for everything. Why can't your mother be?

CAROL:

> 'Cause she doesn't have any cue cards, that's why.

> *FRAN enters with a towel which she gives to ERNIE.*

ERNIE:

> Fran, this is a towel.

FRAN:

> Yes, a towel I use for dusting.

> *ERNIE hands the towel to FRED, who proceeds to dust out the back of the TV.*

JAMIE:

"The Brady Bunch" is a lot of crap.

ERNIE:

What?

JAMIE:

"The Brady Bunch" is a lot of sugar-coated crap
and so is "All in the Family."

ERNIE:

Well, at least the boys in "The Brady Bunch" like
girls. And Archie Bunker wouldn't be caught dead
reading poetry.

FRED:

Who's reading poetry?

ERNIE:

Jamie boy here. I went up to university one time
and caught him reading some crap by a guy called
"Yeast."

JAMIE:

It was by W.B. Yeats, Dad, and it may interest you
to know, I was writing a term paper.

ERNIE:

If that's what they give you to write term papers on,
no wonder you ended up in the Clarke.

FRAN:

Ernie, there's nothing wrong with liking poetry.

FRED:

I dunno, Mom. If Jock caught me reading that stuff,
he'd fire me on the spot.

CAROL:
> What does he know about anything? He thinks
> Mickey Spillaine wrote *Hamlet.*

FRED:
> Well, it's not the kind of thing a man does.

CAROL: *angrily*
> How would you know?

ERNIE:
> Fred's right. What would you think if you saw Matt
> Dillon or Ben Cartwright reading poetry?

CAROL:
> I doubt if they could read.

FRED:
> Of course they can read. If they couldn't, Matt
> Dillon wouldn't be able to read the wanted posters
> right, Dad?

ERNIE:
> Right.

JAMIE:
> He should try a book on acting.

ERNIE:
> Jamie, the Marshall of Dodge City has no time to act.

> *By now the television should be all dusted out
> and the back screwed on again.*

FRED:
> There. Let her rip.

ERNIE: *turning it on*
> Now, let's see . . .

A pause while they all look and then . . .

CAROL:
R.C.A. told us there'd be moments like this.

Silence.

ERNIE:
What the hell did you do to it, Fred? It won't even come on.

FRED:
Me? You're the one who kicked the damn thing.

ERNIE:
What are you talking about? It was still working then. You've buggered it up with that screwdriver.

FRED:
You told me to fix it, Dad.

ERNIE:
I told you to fix it so it would work, dummy. Now thanks to you, I'm out two hundred and fifty bucks.

JAMIE:
Two twenty-five, Dad.

CAROL: *getting up*
Well, come on, Handy Andy, it's time to go.

FRED gets up.

ERNIE:
Don't go yet. You can listen to the game on the radio.

CAROL:
Dad, I'm not feeling very well and anyway, we've got a radio at home.

ERNIE:
Why don't you have a lie down here? Or better still, why don't you and Fred stay overnight? Save the long drive home.

CAROL:
It's not that long.

ERNIE:
You can sleep in your own room. It'll be just like old times.

CAROL:
I don't want to sleep in my own room. I want to sleep in my own apartment.

FRED:
Yeah, if I stay here, Dad, I'd have to get up awfully early.

ERNIE:
It's not good enough for you anymore, is that it?

CAROL:
Look, why do we have to go through this every week? Why are you so hot about us staying overnight? We've got our own place now.

ERNIE:
It beats me how you can pay rent to a perfect stranger when you could live here for practically nothing.

CAROL:
It's nearer to Fred's work.

ERNIE:

>It'd be near enough right here if Fred had stayed on at the plant. But, oh no, he had to change jobs. Didn't even ask my advice.

CAROL:

>Well, goodnight everybody.

ERNIE:

>Wait a minute, Fred. How about one for the road?

FRED:

>No, Dad, I think we'd better go. Carol's tired —

ERNIE:

>You mean my old drinking buddy's gone soft. Eight years of marriage have worn him down.

FRED:

>It's not that.

ERNIE:

>Come here a minute. I want to look at something.

>>*FRED goes over to ERNIE, who examines his face carefully.*

>Yep, I can see 'em as clear as day.

FRED:

>See what?

ERNIE:

>The hole where she puts the ring. What does she do, take it out for good behaviour?

>>*FRED pushes ERNIE away angrily. ERNIE laughs.*

FRED:
>Okay, give me a beer.

CAROL:
>Fred . . .

FRED:
>You shut up!

CAROL:
>Fred, if you're late one more time . . .

FRED:
>I won't be late.

ERNIE:
>What's this about being late?

FRED:
>Oh, Jock got a little sore 'cause I was late once.

CAROL:
>Twice. You were an hour late.

FRED:
>I was not.

FRAN:
>In that case, Fred, maybe you'd better go.

ERNIE:
>Leave the man alone. He's old enough to make up his own mind.

CAROL:
>I bet Sergio's never late.

ERNIE:
>Who's Sergio?

FRED:

A little wop at the garage who's always trying to suck up to Jock.

CAROL:

Yeah, by getting to work on time.

FRED:

How's about that beer, Dad?

ERNIE:

Sure thing. Jamie?

JAMIE:

I'd rather have a cold one.

He exits to the kitchen.

CAROL:

Then I want a scotch and soda.

ERNIE:

No sir, not in your condition.

FRED:

Get her a Pepsi, Mom.

CAROL:

I want a scotch and soda. I'm celebrating.

FRED:

You can celebrate with a Pepsi.

FRAN:

Remember the baby, Carol.

CAROL:

That's why I'm celebrating. And I'm going to do it with a scotch and soda.

FRED:

> Please, Sugar, not tonight.

CAROL:

> What makes it so different from any other night?

> *She exits to the kitchen.*

ERNIE:

> Go with her, Fran.

FRED:

> Yeah, and tell her she better come back here with a Pepsi if she knows what's good for her.

> *FRAN exits.*

ERNIE:

> What's wrong with her, Fred? Doesn't she care about the kid?

FRED:

> Of course, Dad. Why shouldn't she?

ERNIE:

> Her problem with the bottle isn't getting out of hand again, is it?

FRED:

> Well, you know Carol, Dad . . .

ERNIE:

> Yeah, I know Carol. Answer the question.

FRED:

> Look . . . Carol may have overdone it with the booze once or twice, but it's not a problem.

ERNIE:

> That's why we had to have her stomach pumped out last Easter, eh?

FRED:

> That could have happened to anyone.

ERNIE:

> Anyone with a drinking problem. What are you doing about it, Fred?

FRED:

> Well, we talk about it. We talk a lot about it . . .

ERNIE:

> And? . . .

FRED:

> And I tell her not to drink.

ERNIE:

> And that's why she's in the kitchen right now getting a scotch and soda.

FRED:

> I told her to get a Pepsi.

ERNIE:

> Yeah, and you scared her shitless, didn't you? Old fearless Fred.

FRED:

> Well, whaddaya want me to do?

ERNIE:

> I want you to be firm. Be a man.

FRED:

> I am a man! Tell that to Jamie, Dad. It's him you're not sure about.

ERNIE:
> Leave Jamie out of this.

FRED:
> I'll bet you ten bucks he's not even gonna call that Cindy broad.

ERNIE:
> Whaddaya mean?

FRED:
> He's scared to call her. He doesn't want to go out with Cindy. He'd rather go out with Lenny.

ERNIE:
> What the hell are you talking about? *Pause.*
> Okay, we'll see. You got yourself a bet.

> *They shake hands just as JAMIE, FRAN and CAROL enter. CAROL has a scotch and soda.*

FRED:
> That's not Pepsi, Carol.

CAROL:
> Go to the head of the class, Freddy.

FRED:
> Damnit, woman, I told you to get a Pepsi!

CAROL:
> And that's why I got a scotch and soda.

ERNIE:
> Fran, you were supposed to see that she got a Pepsi.

FRAN:
> But Ernie, she got it before I could . . .

ERNIE: *angrily*
   Don't you ever do as your told, woman? EVER!

FRAN: *frightened*
   But Ernie, I . . .

ERNIE:
   ARE YOU SO DAMN STUPID THAT YOU CAN'T
   UNDERSTAND ENGLISH ANYMORE? ARE YOU?

JAMIE: *enraged*
   Stop it!

ERNIE:
   What was that?

JAMIE:
   You heard me.

FRAN: *concerned*
   Jamie, calm down.

ERNIE:
   Now see here, Mr. Big Man on Campus, this is my
   house and I will say and do as I please in it and as
   long as you are living here you will keep your trap
   shut and do as you're told. Do I make myself
   perfectly clear? Do I?

CAROL:
   Yes, Dad, I think they both got the message.

FRED: *to CAROL*
   Now see what you've done?

CAROL:
   Me?

FRED:

> Yes, you. None of this would have happened if you'd done as you were told. Now no more scotch and soda and that's final.

> *JAMIE gets up to leave.*

> Where are you going, kid?

JAMIE:

> Upstairs to read. You mind?

FRED:

> Of course I mind. It's family night. We haven't seen you since Christmas.

ERNIE:

> Fred's right. Look, Jamie, I didn't mean to yell at you. You know what I'm like. Come on back and sit down.

JAMIE:

> Dad, the TV's broken and I don't feel like talking.

FRED:

> Hey, Dad, I was just wondering. Maybe it's the aerial.

ERNIE:

> Could be. I'll have it checked in the morning. Come on, Jamie, Carol wants to talk to you, don't you, Carol?

FRED:

> If we had a ladder and a flashlight we could check it right now.

FRAN:

> Just where are you going to get a ladder this time of night?

FRED:

There must be one around somewhere. Don't the Wilsons next door have one?

FRAN:

It's pitch black outside. You'll fall off the roof, for God's sake.

FRED:

Mom, it's a flat roof. No one will get hurt.

CAROL:

Don't be stupid, Fred. You can hear the game on the kitchen radio.

FRED:

Just drink your scotch, Sugar, and keep your dumb opinions to yourself. Whaddaya say, Dad?

ERNIE:

I'm with you. Fran, get the flashlight and then come on outside and hold the ladder. Take it easy, kids, we'll be right back.

They exit. FRAN exits to the kitchen and a moment later enters again carrying a flashlight.

FRAN: *crossing to the front hall*
Boys will be boys.

FRAN exits.

CAROL looks at JAMIE for a moment, then gets up, exits to the kitchen and reappears with the bottle of scotch. She pours herself another drink.

JAMIE:

Hadn't you better go easy on that stuff?

CAROL:
> Why? I like it.

JAMIE:
> Is it worth getting sick just to get even with Fred?

CAROL:
> That has nothing to do with it. I'm celebrating the death of television.

JAMIE:
> I thought you said you were celebrating the baby.

CAROL:
> Same thing.

JAMIE:
> What do you mean?

CAROL:
> Do you care about the baby, Jamie? Are you so hot to be an uncle?

JAMIE:
> No, I'd just like to know how it happened. I thought you were on the pill.

CAROL:
> Well, old Numbnuts couldn't get it up for over three months so I started to forget. Then one day I'm sitting there in the kitchen eating an apple and Fred staggers in pissed out of his mind. They'd had a party at the garage to celebrate Fred's tightening his first screw by himself or something, I don't know. Anyway, I'm sitting there eating my apple and in walks the great lover. First he tells me to make him a ham sandwich. I tell him to go fuck himself. Since he's probably been doing that for the last three months, he decides he wants a change of pace. So

before I know it, I'm on the floor, minus my knickers, and passion's plaything is bouncing up and down on top of me like a jack-in-the-box. Didn't even get to finish my apple. *Pause.* I thought alcohol was a depressant. *Pause.* Of course, if you're like Fred, the only way to go is up.

JAMIE:

Dad wants to be a patriarch like Will Geer on "The Waltons."

CAROL:

Well, both Dad and Will Geer can go piss up a tree. And the next time Freddikins gets horny, he can go play in the bathroom.

JAMIE:

You should never have married the jerk.

CAROL:

Easy to say, Jamie. But remember, I needed to get away from Dad then just as badly as you do right now.

JAMIE:

Why's he so hot about me getting married?

CAROL:

Because he believes in equality. He thinks everybody should be equally miserable.

JAMIE:

Are you and Fred equally miserable?

CAROL:

Well, we're not exactly "McMillan and Wife," are we? But then I guess no one else is either.

JAMIE:
    I still don't understand why you married him.

CAROL:
    Would you believe that at one time I loved him? You
    know, when he wasn't performing for Dad he could
    really be very sweet. Dumb, I'll grant you, but sweet.
    Now whenever he's away from Dad or Jock it's like
    he's rehearsing for them or something. God, especially
    these last three months.

        Slight pause.

JAMIE:
    Carol, is that Fred's baby?

CAROL:
    Are you going to call Cindy?

JAMIE:
    What do you think?

CAROL:
    Dad will bug the ass off you until you do. I know,
    tell him you have a girlfriend.

JAMIE:
    I don't.

CAROL:
    So tell him you have. It will shut him up for a while.

JAMIE:
    I can't lie to him.

CAROL:
    Why not? Fred and I do it all the time.

JAMIE:
Because I can't, that's why.

CAROL:
Suit yourself. *Pause.* Jamie, you have been laid,
haven't you? You aren't a virgin after all this time?

JAMIE:
You're beginning to sound like Fred.

CAROL:
No. Fred says, "Yes, Dad," and "I'm sorry, Dad."
I gave that up a long time ago.

She pours herself another drink.

JAMIE:
Look, Carol, I really think you've had enough.
What's say we put this away?

He reaches for the bottle, but she snatches it.

CAROL:
What's say we don't, eh?

JAMIE:
You're just going to make trouble.

CAROL:
Who gives a shit?

JAMIE:.
If you don't care about the kid, care about yourself.

CAROL:
Tell me about your love life.

JAMIE:
Tell me about yours.

CAROL:
> Meaning what?

JAMIE:
> Meaning you didn't answer my question. Is that
> Fred's baby?

CAROL:
> How's Lenny?

> *Pause.*

JAMIE:
> He's okay, I guess.

CAROL:
> You guess? I never hear you talk about him anymore.
> Has Dad ever met him?

JAMIE: *cautiously*
> Yes.

CAROL:
> What does he think of him?

JAMIE:
> I don't know.

CAROL:
> Jamie?

JAMIE:
> What?

CAROL:
> Are you gonna tell me what happened or do I have
> to guess?

JAMIE:

>What happened? When?

CAROL:

>What made you flip out?

JAMIE:

>I didn't flip out. I was a little depressed, that's all.

CAROL:

>So how come you landed in the Clarke?

JAMIE:

>I told you how. Strain.

CAROL:

>The strain of what? Who caused the strain?

JAMIE:

>No one.

CAROL:

>That's bullshit. *Pause.* What does the doctor say?

JAMIE:

>That's confidential, Carol.

CAROL:

>Don't give me that crap, Jamie. I'm your sister.
>*Pause.* It has something to do with Dad, hasn't it?
>*Slight pause.* Dad and Lenny.

JAMIE:

>Look, no one said . . .

CAROL:

>Jamie, please, it's been a long hard day and I'm
>tired. If someone doesn't tell me what the hell's
>going on around here, I just might flip out myself.

JAMIE:
>What do you want to know for?

CAROL:
>Because you're one of the few things I have to hang
>on to, that's why.

JAMIE:
>Therapy, eh?

>>*She starts to pour another drink. JAMIE takes
>>the bottle away from her.*

>>*Silence.*

>The doctor wants me to tell Dad to fuck off.

CAROL:
>Hallelujah! Are you going to?

JAMIE:
>I don't know yet. I don't even know why I came
>back.

CAROL:
>What happened, Jamie? Please tell me.

JAMIE: *after a pause, where he struggles to find the words*
>You see, Carol, things were really great at Mac. I
>really dug it. It's the first time in my life I felt free to
>be myself. No hassles. Nobody making you feel
>obligated. No one pulling at you to be what they
>wanted. You came and you went. I never knew
>anything like it before, Carol. It was beautiful.
>Especially with Lenny. *Pause.* I guess I always
>knew how he felt about me. But he never pushed it.
>He just contented himself with being my friend. It
>was like that five days a week and then Friday would
>roll around and . . .

CAROL:
> Up would come Daddy . . .

JAMIE:
> For no reason at all other than to spy on me and
> pressure me into doing what he wanted me to do.
> Which usually meant going out and getting drunk.
> Once I even asked him if he'd mind not coming up
> so often, just maybe once or twice a month. He got
> mad and said just because I was at university didn't
> mean I was too good for him. I felt guilty and said
> I was sorry. And so it continued. Once I even had
> to take him to a sorority party. And then he met
> Lenny.

CAROL:
> What happened?

JAMIE:
> Lenny and I were sitting in my room talking when
> Dad as usual barged in. He invited us both out for a
> beer. That was okay, but all during the evening, he
> didn't take his eyes off Lenny. Then he started to
> make the usual suggestions about going to pick up
> girls. He started asking Lenny what kind of girls he
> preferred and had he ever been laid. At this point I
> persuaded Dad it was time to leave and he dropped
> the subject. Then we were walking home and we were
> passing this . . . I don't want to talk about it any-
> more.

CAROL:
> C'mon, Jamie.

JAMIE:
> No.

CAROL:
> Jamie, please.

JAMIE:
   I said no.

CAROL:
   Please, honey, I've got to know.

JAMIE:
   We were passing this dress shop and Dad asked
   Lenny if he liked the dress in the window. Lenny
   said it was alright. Then Dad said he'd buy him
   that dress if . . .

   JAMIE struggles for control.

   If he'd get the hell away from his son and stay
   away. I tried to say something but Dad told me to
   shut the fuck up, he'd handle this. He pinned Lenny
   up against the glass and said if he ever caught him
   mooning around me again, he and Fred were going to
   come down and beat the shit out of him. Lenny just
   ran down the street, looking like he'd been run over
   by a truck. The next day I tried to find him to apolo-
   gize for what happened. He admitted it was true. He
   was in love with me. He wanted to sleep with me. In
   that case, I said, we couldn't be friends anymore. He
   started crying. Oh my God, Carol, how he cried.
   And I felt sick. He tried to phone me. Tried to see
   me. It got so I was afraid to walk on campus for fear
   of running into him. Then he gave up. When finally
   I did see him I knew he hated my guts.

CAROL:
   Is that what put you in the Clarke?

JAMIE:
   Yeah, probably. That, and other things . . .

115

ERNIE: *off*
>Forget about the ladder, Fran. You can put it away in the morning.

>*ERNIE, FRAN and FRED enter.*

CAROL:
>Find anything?

FRED:
>Not a damn thing.

CAROL:
>Didn't think you would. Want another beer?

FRED:
>Don't mind if I do, Sugar. Why the change of heart?

CAROL:
>No change of heart. You've been saying no to me and yes to Daddy all evening, so I thought I'd try a little reverse psychology.

>*FRED opens another beer. Then he notices the scotch.*

FRED:
>What's that doing there?

CAROL:
>The Avon Lady brought it. *Pause.* Ding-dong.

FRED:
>That's your second drink.

CAROL:
>Wrong again, Freddikins. It's my third.

ERNIE:
>   Jamie, why didn't you stop her?

CAROL:
>   Oh, Daddy, he tried. He tried his bestest, but you
>   know what a bitch I can be.

FRED:
>   Every night. Every fuckin' night, it's the same thing!

CAROL:
>   Now watch your language, Freddy.

FRED:
>   You don't give a shit about the baby, do you?

CAROL:
>   Have a potato chip.

>   *She holds out the bowl to him.*

FRED:
>   Do you?

CAROL:
>   Have a potato chip, you stupid prick!

>   *She throws the chips in his face.*

FRED:
>   Okay, Carol, the party's over.

>   *He snatches the glass from her hand and grabs
>   the bottle.*

ERNIE:
>   Take it easy, Fred. Remember her condition.

FRED:

Fuck her condition! She's drunk! A baby on the way and she's pissed out of her goddamned skull. Just like she's been ever since she told me!

ERNIE:

Okay, Fred, calm down.

FRED:

Sorry, Dad.

CAROL:

You see, Dad, Freddikins is sorry. He won't do it again. He'll just sit there and be a good wittle boy.

FRED: *enraged*
Goddamn bitch!

> *He lunges for her. JAMIE and ERNIE grab FRED. FRAN moves to protect CAROL.*

JAMIE:

Stop it!

ERNIE:

Cut it out, Fred!

> *FRED keeps on struggling.*

FRED:

Always making me feel like nothing! Like shit.

> *ERNIE and JAMIE manage to push him back into his chair.*

CAROL:
YOU ARE SHIT!!

ERNIE:
> Shut up!

> *Pause.*

CAROL:
> I need another drink.

FRAN: *angrily*
> You've had enough.

ERNIE:
> Oh, get her another drink if it'll keep her quiet. If
> anything happens to the baby, it'll be on her head.

FRAN:
> Look at this mess! Some people around here think I
> do housework just to pass the time. Well, I don't.

ERNIE:
> Fran, just go and get the drink!

FRAN:
> If you'd spent your money on a TV that works,
> Ernie, instead of junk like that dog, this never would
> have happened.

ERNIE:
> FRAN!!

> *She exits. He turns to CAROL and FRED.*

> Now what the hell's going on? Fred told me every-
> thing was alright between you two.

CAROL:
> It used to be. *Pause.* Way back when.

ERNIE:

    So what's the problem?

CAROL:

    So will you tell him Freddy or shall I?

FRED:

    There's nothing to tell.

CAROL:

    Oh yes there is. Shall I tell him I'm going to have a
    miscarriage?

        On this last word, FRAN enters with the soda
        water and stops dead.

FRED:

    For Chrissake, Carol!!

FRAN:

    Miscarriage? Who had a miscarriage?

CAROL:

    Soda water. Will you get me a drink, for Chrissake!

ERNIE:

    Would someone please tell me what the hell's going
    on?

FRAN:

    Something happened at the doctor's today, didn't it?

FRED: *frightened*

    Nothing happened.

CAROL:

    Yes, it did, Freddy boy, and you know it.

ERNIE: *climbing the wall*
 WHAT HAPPENED?

CAROL:
 Well, let me put it this way, Dad. It's gonna be a
 long time before you're a patriarch.

FRED: *panic-stricken*
 Don't listen to her, Dad, she's drunk. Wanna go
 home, Sugar? Let's go home.

CAROL:
 It's too late for that, Booby. It's "Bombs Away"
 time.

ERNIE:
 What do you mean? You're not pregnant? It's a
 false alarm?

CAROL:
 Oh, I'm pregnant enough alright.

FRED: *pleading*
 Carol!

CAROL:
 But I decided to get unpregnant. I'm going to have
 an abortion.

 *Dead thunderstruck silence. FRED collapses
 into a chair. FRAN looks as if she's going to
 faint.*

ERNIE:
 The hell you are! You'll have an abortion over my
 dead body!

CAROL:

Well, you better start making arrangements with the undertaker now because I have an appointment with the doctor on Saturday.

FRAN:

Carol, why do you want to have an abortion?

CAROL:

Because I don't want the goddamn baby, that's why!

FRED:

Yeah, 'cause it would mean you wouldn't be able to sit on your ass watching TV and boozing all day.

CAROL:

No, Casanova, because it means I'd have a harder time getting rid of you.

FRED:

Well, that's too bad, 'cause you ain't getting rid of me and you ain't having no goddamned abortion. You're gonna do as you're bloody well told!

CAROL:

No, I'm not, so cut the stupid tough-guy act.

FRED:

It's no act, Carol! We've been trying for eight years and now when I finally hit the target, if you think you're gonna . . .

CAROL:

Hit the target! Hit the target! Okay, Buffalo Bill, you've hit the target. Here's your prize.

She hands him the plaster dog. FRED holds it for a moment, stunned.

FRAN:
Carol, why does the doctor want to abort it?

CAROL:
Because he says I'm very depressed. I'm in no condition to be a mother.

ERNIE:
Nonsense. You gotta good home, a husband, three square meals a day. What have you got to be depressed about?

CAROL:
Maybe it's because I keep missing "Mod Squad."

FRED:
Dad, she thinks telling that doctor a big sob story will get her out of having a kid. Well, it won't, 'cause I'm going down there myself first thing in the morning to tell him it's all off.

ERNIE:
You know what I think? I think this quack is looking for a way to pad his bill.

FRED:
Yeah, I wouldn't be surprised. Those finks are always trying to squeeze money out of the government.

ERNIE:
I think you oughtta change doctors. Help yourself to another beer, Fred.

FRED nods and ERNIE starts opening the beer.

CAROL:
I am not changing doctors and I'm having the abortion.

FRED looks like he's going to go crazy.

ERNIE:

> Carol's just upset. Just a little stage fright. Reminds me of an episode I saw on "Marcus Welby." This girl was upset and wanted an abortion, but Dr. Welby . . .

JAMIE:

> Dad, for Chrissake! Will you forget the TV for once!

ERNIE:

> It's the same thing.

JAMIE:

> No, it isn't!

CAROL:

> No, it isn't because this girl's having the abortion.

FRED:

> Like hell! We're gonna make Dad a patriarch like I promised.

CAROL:

> All patriarchs are faggots, Fred.

ERNIE:

> Carol, just calm down and think about what you're doing.

CAROL:

> I've been thinking about it for two months and on Saturday I'm going to do something about it.

FRAN:

> Ernie, if that's what Carol wants, maybe . . .

ERNIE:

> Maybe you better just keep out of this.

124

FRAN:
  She's my daughter too!

ERNIE:
  I know she's your daughter, but I'll handle this, thank you. I think I'm better qualified than you.

CAROL:
  When did you have your abortion, Dad?

ERNIE: *parental*
  Carol, you have that abortion and you'll never set foot in this house again.

FRAN: *frightened*
  Ernie . . .

ERNIE:
  I'll disown you. You hear?

Pause, while CAROL finishes her drink.

CAROL:
  Best offer I've had all day.

She starts toward the door. ERNIE is puzzled at first and then frightened.

ERNIE:
  Look, Carol, I'm sorry. I didn't mean it.

CAROL:
  I'm still going through with it, Dad.

ERNIE:
  Maybe the doctor knows best after all. I don't know. We can talk about it some more tomorrow.

CAROL:

    I'm all through talking.

ERNIE:

    Well, come back and sit down. Please. *Pause.*
    Pour her another drink, Fran.

        CAROL takes off her coat and returns to her
        seat. FRAN pours a drink. FRED is furious.

FRED:

    What about all that shit about being a patriarch?

ERNIE:

    What about it?

FRED:

    Well, have you given up on that idea already?

ERNIE:

    I haven't given up on anything. It just means I'll have
    to wait. There's always Jamie, you know.

FRED:

    Jamie!

JAMIE:

    What's so funny?

FRED:

    Dad, you're not serious!

ERNIE:

    Look, Jamie is more of a man than you'll ever be and
    I'm gonna prove it. *Slight pause.* Jamie, it's time
    to call Cindy.

JAMIE:

    So go ahead and call her.

ERNIE:

    Don't be a smart ass. You know what I mean.

JAMIE:

    Not interested.

FRED:

    What's the matter, you scared?

CAROL:

    You shut your mouth, Fred!

FRED:

    Go to hell, Sugar. *To JAMIE.* Are you scared, Jamie? She sounds like a pretty hot little number. Does that scare you, kid?

JAMIE:

    Why should it? It isn't three months since I've had an erection.

ERNIE:

    Come on, that's enough! Knock it off.

FRED:

    I think you made a mistake, Dad. You shouldn't have gotten him Cindy's phone number. You should've gotten him an office boy's. A cute little office boy with a nice ass named Lenny.

JAMIE: *enraged*
    GO TO HELL!

CAROL: *to FRED*
    YOU BASTARD! YOU SON OF A BITCH!

JAMIE: *turning on his father*
    You had to tell him, didn't you? You had to brag about it to your best buddy.

ERNIE:

>I was protecting my son.

JAMIE:

>It's not from Lenny I need protection, Dad!

ERNIE:

>That little pervert would have had you in the hay if I hadn't stepped in.

JAMIE:

>So who asked you to?

FRED:

>He's right, Dad. Maybe Jamie didn't even want protection. You probably broke up a beautiful friendship or whatever people like Lenny and Jamie call it.

ERNIE:

>Yeah, Fred, the two lovebirds were probably making it in the hay long before I broke it up . . . If I did break it up.

JAMIE:

>GIVE ME THE NUMBER!

ERNIE:

>No. You aren't fit for Cindy to wipe her ass on.

JAMIE: *out of control*

>GIVE ME THE FUCKING NUMBER!

>>*JAMIE grabs the number where ERNIE has left it for him on the table earlier. He goes to the phone and dials.*

FRED: *taking ERNIE aside*
I sweated my guts for you, got drunk with you, went bowling, took a lot of shit from everyone at work. Now when I finally give you what you want, you're gonna let her get rid of it?

ERNIE:
Not now, Fred. Later.

FRED:
To hell with later! You've been waiting for this kid for eight goddamn years. Always teasing, always goading me, always asking me when I was gonna come up with the goods.

ERNIE: *his eyes on JAMIE, pushing FRED aside*
Alright, Fred. Will you shut up!

> *Seeing that it's hopeless, FRED lapses into silence.*

JAMIE:
Hello? *Pause.* Is Cindy . . . *Pause.* Just a moment, please. *To ERNIE.* It's the fire department, Dad. They want to know where the fire is.

> *ERNIE grabs the phone.*

ERNIE:
Hello? What? *Pause.* Sorry, wrong number.

> *He hangs up. JAMIE and CAROL laugh loudly.*

Okay you two, clam up. *Pause.* I said CLAM UP!

> *They stop laughing. He turns to JAMIE.*

You dialed the wrong number . . .

JAMIE:
>Dial it yourself.

He hands him the number.

ERNIE:
>Or someone's farting around. She has a younger
>brother, you know.

He dials.

>Hello? Look, quit fooling around. You can get into
>a lot of trouble for . . . *Pause.* Okay, okay, I'm
>sorry. *Pause.* I know. *Pause.* We were mistaken.
>*Pause.* I said I was sorry, didn't I?

He hangs up.

ERNIE:
>Goddamn bitch! Fuckin' little tart! Too good for
>my son, eh? Well, I'll show that little slut!

CAROL:
>Whatever happened to the little lady?

ERNIE:
>Wait till I get hold of that little tramp tomorrow.

FRAN:
>Ernie, don't. It's not worth losing your job over.

ERNIE:
>Fran, the rest of them put her up to this. She hasn't
>got the brains to think of it herself. Probably
>whispered it in her ear while they groped her during
>coffee break. Well, I'll get even with those fuckers.

FRAN:
>Ernie, please don't do anything.

130

CAROL:
Mom's right. You've been there twenty-five years.

ERNIE:

Yeah, twenty-five lousy, stinkin' years those bastards
have pissed on me behind my back.

FRAN:
So you'll just have to act like nothing's happened.

ERNIE:
Fran! . . .

FRAN:
Show them you're a bigger man than they are.

ERNIE:
Fran, that little . . .

FRAN: *grabbing him*
Ernie, she's not worth it!

*She sits him by her on the sofa and takes his
hand, calming him down.*

ERNIE:
Maybe you're right. *Pause.* Well, don't worry about
Cindy, Jamie. There's lots of other fish in the sea.
Pause. Fred, what about Brenda, the nurse?

FRED:
Who?

ERNIE:
You know, Brenda. The nurse at the plant.

FRED:
She's pushing thirty, Dad.

ERNIE:

>So? Lots of guys go out with older women.

JAMIE:

>I don't.

ERNIE:

>But they're experienced. They can teach you things.

JAMIE:

>I'm not interested in Brenda, the nurse.

ERNIE:

>What have you got against women?

JAMIE:

>NOTHING!

ERNIE:

>Fine. I'll talk to her tomorrow.

CAROL:

>You do that, Daddy dear, and you'll be in deep shit
>up to your lower lip.

ERNIE:

>What are you talking about?

CAROL:

>Well, according to Numbnuts here, you're not exactly
>the apple of her eye.

ERNIE:

>What's she saying, Fred?

FRED: *frightened*

>I don't know, Dad. She's drunk.

CAROL:

I'm saying that Brenda, the nurse, and the rest of the girls are getting a little sick of Robin, the wonder stud, bugging the ass off them while they're trying to work.

ERNIE:

That's not true!

CAROL:

In fact, if you bother them anymore, they're gonna lodge a complaint with the management.

ERNIE:

I only try to be friendly.

CAROL:

Friendly?! You know what they call you behind your back?

FRED:

Sugar . . .

CAROL:

Shut up! Ernie, the mauler.

ERNIE:

Nonsense. I invite them out for coffee once in a while. What's wrong with that?

CAROL:

Yeah, well, she misunderstood you alright . . . You proposition them. They say they can't trust you unless you're across the room, and a big room at that. You even grossed out Freddy here. It got so bad he was embarrassed to be around you. That's why he changed jobs.

FRAN:
>
> Ernie Dinsdale!

ERNIE:
>
> She's exaggerating.

CAROL:
>
> Exaggerating, eh? What about the time you followed that sixteen year old kid into the storeroom and shut the door?

ERNIE:
>
> That was just a misunderstanding.

CAROL:
>
> Yeah, well she misunderstood you, all right . . . You scared the shit out of her. Fred had to do some fast talking to keep her from tellin' the cops, much less the manager.

FRAN:
>
> Ernie Dinsdale! How could you!

ERNIE:
>
> I thought she liked me.

FRAN:
>
> A man your age running after sixteen year old girls!

ERNIE:
>
> Yeah, a man my age! You're bloody right, a man my age! And what the hell are you gonna do about it, eh, woman?

FRAN:
>
> But Ernie, you're a married man!

ERNIE:

> Oh sure, and look what I married, a real ball of fire, who hands it out once a month with all the enthusiasm of a wet mop.

FRAN:

> Oh, Ernie.

ERNIE:

> Don't you "Oh, Ernie" me, you whiney bitch! I was always nothing to you. Nothing! Just a poor slob who doles out money while you make an alcoholic out of his daughter and a Christ knows what out of his son.

JAMIE: *exploding*
> SHUT UP!

> *JAMIE leaps from his chair, grabs a beer bottle and lunges at ERNIE.*

CAROL: *frightened*
> Jamie!

FRED: *grabbing JAMIE*
> Knock it off.

ERNIE:

> You're crazy, boy, you're really crazy. They ought to put you in the Clarke and throw away the key.

JAMIE:

> Shut the fuck up, old man! Just shut up!

ERNIE: *turning away*
> Aw, to hell with you.

JAMIE:

LISTEN! Why do you think I went away to university? Not for their courses, Dad. It was to get away from you. All my life has been one big attempt to get away from you. But it didn't work, did it? You had to come up week after week, making a fool of yourself with all my friends, inviting yourself to all the parties, propositioning girls, picking on people like Lenny for being what they were. You weren't even considerate enough to leave me alone during exams. You had to be up there every week to make a man of me. Your kind of man. Your idea of a man. By the way, Dad, how much did you try to pay Cindy?

ERNIE:

I don't know what you're talking about.

JAMIE:

I'm talking about the fifty bucks you paid that sorority girl to get me into the sack.

ERNIE:

That's a damn lie!

JAMIE:

Dad, she gave me the fifty dollars to give back to you! It's upstairs in my wallet.

Long pause. CAROL pours herself another drink.

CAROL:

Oh, you're a real treasure, Ernie. No one's safe from you. You have to control everybody. Me, mother, Fred, everybody. You've gotta mold them into your idea of some stupid idea you learned off that bloody TV. And if they won't fit into your precious mold, you crush them and destroy them like you've crushed

Fred here. Getting on his back about having babies.
Well, he tried. He tried his damndest. And the
harder he tried, the harder it was to do it. So now
he's failed and you spit him out like chewed-up
tobacco. You tried to turn me into a Donna Reed
or a Sally Fields or whatever dumb fantasy you had
in your mind. You pushed and pressured me until I
went running straight to the first escape hatch I
could find . . . And a fat lot of good that did, eh?
And mother. Who was she suppose to be, Ernie?
Harriet Nelson? Or Lucille Ball? And now it's
Jamie's turn. You want him to be a ladies man like
that creep Banacek, whose philosophy is find 'em,
fuck 'em, and forget 'em. No tenderness, no love,
just get in there and bang away. Anything else and
there's something wrong. The guy's not normal. He's
queer or impotent or some such goddamn thing.
And all because it's not according to the script! You
won't be satisfied until everyone performs for you at
the click of a switch, like on this bloody TV. Well,
no more, Ernie. This show is cancelled. The ratings
are the lowest in TV history, 'cause there's only one
viewer . . . You!

ERNIE:

You . . . get the hell out of here, you lush, and take
your crazy faggot brother with you!

CAROL:

Don't worry. We're going. As for Fred, he's all
yours. Hear that, Freddy boy? Don't bother coming
home tomorrow because I'm having the locks
changed first thing in the morning. Come on, Jamie.

*They exit. ERNIE and FRAN and FRED sit in
silence. The front door slams offstage. A
moment's pause and then . . .*

FRED:
>   Hey, Dad, it's working.

>   *The noise of a Toronto-Boston hockey game gradually fills the room. No one is interested except for FRED. Slowly, FRAN rises and makes a move to clean up, but changes her mind.*

FRAN:
>   Well, I'm going to bed.

>   *She looks at ERNIE for a moment and then exits. Toronto scores a goal. FRED moves around to a chair close to the TV and pulls it up in front of the screen. He gets the potato chips and settles in to watch the game.*

FRED: *suddenly remembering*
>   Hey, Dad, I just remembered, I owe you ten bucks.

>   *Pause. ERNIE does not respond.*

Dad?

>   *Still no response. Trying to make contact.*

Gee, Dad, I didn't know you were a Boston fan . . .

>   *The hockey game continues.*

>   *Slow fade.*

TALONBOOKS — PLAYS IN PRINT 1976

Colours in the Dark — James Reaney
The Ecstasy of Rita Joe — George Ryga
Captives of the Faceless Drummer — George Ryga
Crabdance — Beverley Simons
Listen to the Wind — James Reaney
Ashes for Easter & Other Monodramas — David Watmough
Esker Mike & His Wife, Agiluk — Herschel Hardin
Sunrise on Sarah — George Ryga
Walsh — Sharon Pollock
Apple Butter & Oth　　　．ｊ　ｎ　　　　ｍ　　ames Reaney
The Factory Lab Anthology —　ᴜ　　　　　　　　　-d.
The Trial of Jean-Baptiste M. — Ro.
Battering Ram — David Freeman
Hosanna — Michel Tremblay
Les Belles Soeurs — Michel Tremblay
API 2967 — Robert Gurik
You're Gonna Be Alright Jamie Boy — David Freeman
Bethune — Rod Langley
Preparing — Beverley Simons
Forever Yours Marie-Lou — Michel Tremblay
En Pièces Détachées — Michel Tremblay
Lulu Street — Ann Henry
Three Plays by Eric Nicol — Eric Nicol
Fifteen Miles of Broken Glass — Tom Hendry
Bonjour, là, Bonjour — Michel Tremblay
Jacob's Wake — Michael Cook
On the Job — David Fennario
Sqrieux-de-Dieu — Betty Lambert
Some Angry Summer Songs — John Herbert
The Execution — Marie-Claire Blais
Tiln & Other Plays — Michael Cook
Great Wave of Civilization — Herschel Hardin
La Duchesse de Langeais & Other Plays — Michel Tremblay
Have — Julius Hay